Louisiana Temptations

Recipes from
Louisiana Farm Bureau Women

This cookbook is a collection of our favorite recipes,
which are not necessarily original recipes.

Published by
Louisiana Farm Bureau Federation, Inc.
P.O. Box 95004
9516 Airline Highway
Baton Rouge, Louisiana 70895-9004
504-922-6200

Designed, Edited, and Manufactured by
Favorite Recipes® Press
P.O. Box 305142
Nashville, Tennessee 37230
1-800-358-0560

Library of Congress Number: 96-84999
ISBN: 0-9652035-0-6

Manufactured in the United States of America
First Printing: 1996 20,000 copies

Cover: Cooled by oak trees and gentle breezes of the Tchefuncte River, the front porch of this home in Madisonville, Lousiana, raises the hope of an invitation to enjoy what the owners have lovingly crafted.

Photograph by Judy Jacobs, Baton Rouge, LA

Dedication

The Louisiana Farm Bureau Women's Committee's mission is to develop leadership for women, promote agriculture and develop public understanding of the value and need of agriculture. This cookbook is dedicated to the Louisiana Farm Bureau Women—deepest appreciation for the great strides you have made and for a job well done.

Cookbook Committee

Mrs. Glen (Mindy) Hetzel, Chairman
3138 Crochet Road
Jennings, Louisiana 70546

Mrs. Evelyn Bieber, First Vice-Chairman
8380 White Oak Highway
Branch, Louisiana 70516

Mrs. Cecil (Linda) Williams, Second Vice-Chairman
P.O. Box 61
Keithville, Louisiana 71047

Mrs. George (Denise) Hymel, Third Vice-Chairman
117 Jefferson Highway
Gramercy, Louisiana 70052

Mrs. Daniel (Genevieve) Lyons, Secretary-Treasurer
1438 Jessie Richard Road
Church Point, Louisiana 70525

Foreword, 6

Contributors, 8

Southern Starters, 9
(Appetizers & Beverages)

Gumbos & Greens, 27
(Soups & Salads)

Delta Delights, 53
(Meats, Game & Poultry)

Bayou Bounty, 95
(Fish & Seafood)

French Market Basket, 121
(Vegetables & Side Dishes)

Dough for It, 155
(Breads)

Sweet Dreams, 165
(Cakes & Pies)

Forbidden Indulgences, 191
(Candy, Cookies & Desserts)

Nutritional Profiles, 225

Index, 234

Order Information, 239

Foreword

The temptations of Louisiana are as varied and rich as those who relish them. The allure of the swampland, its cypress trees draped in the mosses of time; the mysteriousness and sometimes wonder generated by the Cajuns and their culture.

But the most tempting of all the Bayou State has to offer is its cuisine.

Food and its preparation have been elevated to art in the hearts and minds of all those who have prepared Louisiana's bountiful harvest over the decades. From the exquisite seafood and rice dishes of South Louisiana, hearty beef dishes from the northwest, to the down-home cooking of corn bread, grits and greens of cotton country in the Northeast Delta, cooking, Louisiana style, is like no other.

And within these pages you'll find ***Louisiana Temptations*** of every kind. From the traditional appeal of a Wednesday night meat loaf to a breezy Saturday afternoon of poke salad and a glass of iced tea, it's all here.

Many of the recipes you'll find are as delicious as they are original. The blend of cultures from across the world who call Louisiana home have stirred up a pot for every palate.

There's a taste of Creole New Orleans, dishes influenced by the Spanish and French. Images of cobblestone streets, row houses in the garden district appear. The aroma of a roux permeates the heavy summer air. It's a shrimp Creole for dinner, served in heirloom crockery on a table that always, *always*, includes candlesticks. And if you listen carefully, you can almost hear the revelers of Mardi Gras, while never taking your eyes off the platter of pecan pralines for dessert.

Then there's a generous helping of Acadiana in the heart of Cajun Country. You can smell the aging wood of the cypress supper table as it blends with crawfish in the stewpot. The two wild scents come together as if to say, "Wake up, Evangeline, it's supper time." It's "Maw Maw's" tablecloth, bearing the stains of divine dishes past, and "Paw Paw's" favorite red-handled spoon, to get every drop if you tilt the bowl just right. *Voulez-vous manger avec moi ce soir?* (Would you like to eat with me tonight?)

To Southwest Louisianians, heaven had better have rice and gravy, otherwise some might have to ponder St. Peter's invitation. In a region where rice reigns supreme, this "white gold" is always in the pan. As a bed for all manner of dishes, to a childhood snack of butter-rice, a generous helping always leads to a satisfied slumber.

Along the Delta of Northeast Louisiana it's meals as tried and true as the South herself. Whatever's for lunch, it's served with corn bread and collard greens that have just enough ham to make you think your family has money. That night it's duck, the smell of its roasted flavor carried along by the winds across the Ouachita. "Maybe there's some greens left over from lunch," you think as you move toward the refrigerator.

Northwest Louisiana is a haven of home and hearth. "Homestyle" epitomizes and gives justification to the black-iron skillet. Time is irrelevant, since white gravy has a way of showing up morning, noon and night. Is that chicken-fried steak? This night, grace lasts just a little too long as you flinch for the fork right before that anticipated "Amen."

The Louisiana Farm Bureau Women's Committee is proud to present this collection of recipes from across our great state. It not only showcases our love of good cooking, but stands as a testament to those farmers and ranchers who produce the abundance of food so necessary to nourish not only the body, but the soul, with healthy, hearty meals.

So prepare to be tempted by ***Louisiana Temptations***. Giving in never tasted so good!

Michael J. Danna

Michael Danna
Wakefield (near St. Francisville), Louisiana

Contributors

Michelle Alexander
Robert Alexander
Dolores Ancelet
Vivian Anderson
Dana Bennett
Donnette W. Bennett
Sue Benoit
Wanda Benton
Constance Bieber
Evelyn Bieber
S. Bieber-Speyrer
Courtney Bolding
Joanne Bolding
Linda Bordelon
Alicia Boudreaux
Gayle Boudreaux
Pam Bouillion
Penny Bouquet
Frances Brasher
Margaret Brewster
Betty Jo Brian
Pam Broussard
Jackie Brown
Melissa Brown
Ruth Brown
Lynn Buzhardt
Candy Carlisle
Claire Carlisle
Genevieve Carlisle
Paige Carlisle
Charlotte Castille
Louise Cater
Patty Champlin
Zuba Chrisman
Buddy Cook
Theresa T. Cormier
Sheila Costello
Becky Creel
Vikki Cutrer
Frances Davis
Janell DeRouen
Sheri DeRouen
Margaret Desselle
Thomas Dicharry
Ann Dodson
Lois Dodson
Linda Drain
Sadie Eastman
Yvonne Eastman
Beryl Eisworth
Joan Falgoust
Dianna Fontenot
Angie B. Futch
Nita Gaines
Priscilla Gragg
Patsy Granger
Grace S. Graugnard
Colette Gravois
Darleen Gravois
Jane S. Gravois
Lynette P. Gravois
Lola Griffin
Kay Haley
Leslie Hanks
Dianna Haring
Sherry Harris
Gert Hawkins
Leonard J. Hensgens
Lacey Hetzel
Mindy Hetzel
Edda Hoffpauir
Pam Holloway
Denise Hymel
Shannon Hymel
Stephen Hymel
Judy G. Jacobs
Dean N. Johnson
Jann Jones
Patricia Kincaid
Betty P. Kirby
Adeline Lafleur
Henrietta Landry
Regan Landry
Regina Landry
Reneé L. LaVergne
Victoria Lawrence
Dot O. Leger
Karen Lemoine
Kris Liles
Pam Little
Onietta Loewer
Jann Logan
Bridget Lyons
Genevieve Lyons
Monica Lyons
Cindy D. Martin
Margaret Martinez
Betty A. McDonald
Melba McIntosh
Billie Middleton
Betty Sue Miller
Norma J. Miller
Reynold Minsky
Billie Mitchell
Carole Mitchell
Diann Mitchell
Connie Monroe
James R. Monroe
Gloria T. Moore
Jennie Lee Moore
Katherine Moore
Phyllis G. Moore
Roger V. Moseley
Cherlyon Nesom
Suzzettee Olivier
Marie Ory
Bonnie Pace
Elaine Parker
Maryanna Perryman
Alice Peterson
Betty Petticrew
Jody Pollard
Phyllis Rabalais
Vashti Radzikowski
Codie Ray
Anne Regan
Mrs. Glen Robinson
Patricia G. Roussel
Tammy Rumbaugh
Martha Scanlon
Doris Schexnaydre
Elsie Schexnayder
Sharlee Schexnayder
Anita Schilling
Donna R. Shields
Marie Simon
Erin A. Sirmon
Pearl Slaughter
Betty Smith
Michelle Soileau
Margaret Sorenson
Nettie Spurgeon
Patty Starkey
Tammie Stutts
Raymond Taylor
Jan Thrash
Loretta Treme
Mary Vail
Felton Vickers
Marilyn Wade
Carolyn Walker
Kathy Warren
Brenda Wells
Karen Wild
Jewell Williams
Linda Williams
Mrs. Stuart Williams
H. C. Zaunbrecher
Linda Zaunbrecher
Beverly Zeringue

Southern Starters

Appetizers & Beverages

As you drive by the old Clinton Brick and Mercantile Company, you can't help but be taken by the tractor which stands guard like an aging bulldog. The 1940 John Deer Model D tractor, with its bulky, squatty frame and spiked wheels, belonged to attorney Ian Lindsey's grandfather, a rice farmer from Lascassine, Louisiana. Lindsey is restoring the brickyard store.

Photograph by Michael Danna, Wakefield, LA

Appetizers & Beverages

Beef and Pork Dip, 11
Broccoli Dip, 12
Chile Corn Dip, 13
Crab Meat Dip, 13
Hot Crab Dip, 14
Mock Crab Salad Dip, 14
Crawfish Dip, 15
Easy Crawfish Dip, 15
Layered Shrimp Dip, 16
Shrimp Rémoulade, 17
Seafood Cocktail Spread, 18
Shrimp Spread, 19
Taco Dip, 19
French Bread and Ham Appetizer, 20
Rice Cakes, 20
Sweet Potato Cheese Balls, 21
Tortilla Pinwheels, 22
Waldorf Sandwiches, 23
Cinnamon Pecans, 23
Eggnog, 24
Easy Punch, 24
Yellow Slush Punch, 25
Spiced Tea, 26

Beef and Pork Dip

1 large onion, chopped
1 green bell pepper, chopped
1 tablespoon chopped garlic
8 ounces fresh mushrooms, chopped
2 tablespoons margarine
1 pound ground beef
1 pound ground pork
Salt and pepper to taste
1 pound Velveeta cheese, cubed

Sauté the onion, green pepper, garlic and mushrooms in the margarine in a skillet until tender. Add the ground beef, ground pork, salt and pepper. Cook over low heat until brown, stirring until crumbly; drain. Add the cheese. Cook until the cheese is melted, stirring occasionally. Spoon into a chafing dish. May serve with garlic bagel chips or crackers. Yield: 16 servings.

Penny Bouquet, Baker

Broccoli Dip

1 (10-ounce) package frozen chopped broccoli
1/2 teaspoon salt
1/4 cup water
1 small onion, chopped
2 teaspoons margarine or butter
1 (10-ounce) can cream of mushroom soup
1 (6-ounce) roll garlic cheese, crumbled
1/2 teaspoon salt
1 teaspoon MSG
1/8 teaspoon pepper
1/8 teaspoon Tabasco sauce
1 teaspoon Worcestershire sauce
1 (4-ounce) can mushroom pieces and stems

Cook the broccoli with 1/2 teaspoon salt in the water in a saucepan until tender; drain. Sauté the onion in the margarine in a large skillet. Add the soup, cheese, salt, MSG, pepper, Tabasco sauce and Worcestershire sauce. Cook over medium heat until the cheese melts, stirring occasionally. Add the broccoli. Cook for 1 minute longer, stirring occasionally. Stir in the mushrooms. Cook until heated through. Serve hot with crackers or chips. May add 3/4 cup slivered almonds. Yield: 16 servings.

Henrietta Landry, Elton

Chile Corn Dip

2 (12-ounce) cans Mexicorn
1 cup sour cream
1 cup mayonnaise
10 ounces Cheddar cheese, shredded
1 (4-ounce) can chopped green chiles, drained
3 to 4 jalapeños, chopped
3 green onions, chopped
1/4 teaspoon sugar

Combine the Mexicorn, sour cream, mayonnaise, cheese, green chiles, jalapeños, green onions and sugar in a bowl and mix well. Chill, covered, for several hours to allow the flavors to blend. Serve with large corn chips. Yield: 24 servings.

Dot O. Leger, Rayne

Crab Meat Dip

1 large onion, finely chopped
4 to 5 tablespoons margarine
8 ounces Velveeta cheese, cubed
1 pound frozen lump crab meat, thawed
1 (6-ounce) can crab meat
8 ounces imitation crab meat, finely chopped
1 (10-ounce) can cream of celery soup

Combine the onion and margarine in a microwave-safe dish. Microwave on High for 3 minutes. Stir in the cheese. Microwave for 1 to 2 minutes or until the cheese is melted, stirring occasionally. Add the crab meat and soup. Microwave for 3 to 4 minutes or until heated through, stirring occasionally.
Yield: 16 servings.

Suzzettee Olivier, Port Barre

Hot Crab Dip

1 large onion, chopped
1 rib celery, chopped
1/2 cup butter
2 tablespoons chopped parsley
2 pounds crab meat
1 pound Velveeta cheese, cubed
1 (5-ounce) can evaporated milk
1 (10-ounce) can cream of mushroom soup
1/2 teaspoon garlic powder
2 tablespoons Worcestershire sauce
Salt and pepper to taste

Sauté the onion and the celery in the butter in a large skillet until tender. Add the parsley, crab meat, cheese, evaporated milk, soup, garlic powder, Worcestershire sauce, salt and pepper. Cook for 15 minutes or until the cheese is melted and the mixture is heated through, stirring occasionally. Serve hot with crackers. Yield: 12 servings.

Nettie Spurgeon, Zachary

Mock Crab Salad Dip

3 pounds imitation crab meat
3 bunches green onions, chopped
8 jumbo black olives, chopped
1/2 cup shredded Cheddar cheese
1 cup mayonnaise-type salad dressing
White pepper and black pepper to taste

Rinse the imitation crab meat and pat dry. Cut into bite-size pieces. Combine with the green onions, olives, cheese, salad dressing and pepper in a bowl and mix well. Chill, covered, for 1 hour. Serve with crackers. Yield: 12 servings.

Victoria Lawrence, Amite

Crawfish Dip

2 bunches green onions, chopped
1 bunch parsley, chopped
2 pounds crawfish tails, cooked
1 cup margarine
24 ounces cream cheese, softened
1 (10-ounce) can cream of mushroom soup
3 tablespoons garlic powder

Sauté the green onions, parsley and crawfish in the margarine in a large skillet. Add the cream cheese, soup and garlic powder. Cook over low heat for 20 minutes or until crawfish are cooked through, stirring occasionally. Serve with chips or crackers. Yield: 16 servings.

Anne Regan, Crowley

Easy Crawfish Dip

2 pounds crawfish, coarsely chopped
3 ribs celery, chopped
1 cup chopped onion
1 green bell pepper, chopped
1/2 cup butter
3 (10-ounce) cans cream of mushroom soup
1 cup shredded Cheddar cheese
Red pepper to taste

Cook the crawfish, celery, onion and green pepper in the butter in a 3-quart saucepan until the vegetables are tender and the crawfish are cooked through. Add the soup and cheese. Cook over low heat until the cheese is melted and dip is of serving temperature, stirring occasionally. Stir in the red pepper. Serve with Melba rounds or assorted crackers. Yield: 20 servings.

Denise Hymel, Gramercy

Layered Shrimp Dip

16 ounces fat-free cream cheese, softened
1 tablespoon Worcestershire sauce
2 to 4 cloves of garlic, minced
1 cup fat-free sour cream
8 ounces seafood cocktail sauce
1 pound peeled cooked seasoned shrimp
1 pound mozzarella cheese, shredded
3 to 6 green onions, chopped
1 green bell pepper, chopped
2 tomatoes, peeled, finely chopped

Combine the cream cheese, Worcestershire sauce, garlic and sour cream in a mixer bowl and beat until well blended. Layer the cream cheese mixture, cocktail sauce, shrimp, cheese, green onions, green pepper and tomatoes in a 12-inch platter. Serve with crackers. Yield: 20 servings.

Joan Falgoust, St. James

Shrimp Rémoulade

3 ribs celery, coarsely chopped
1/2 large green bell pepper, coarsely chopped
2 large green onions, coarsely chopped
10 cloves of garlic
3/4 (6-ounce) jar mustard
1 teaspoon horseradish
1 cup vegetable oil
1/2 cup vinegar
1 cup catsup
2 tablespoons Worcestershire sauce
Tabasco sauce, red pepper, paprika and salt to taste
2 quarts peeled cooked shrimp

Combine the celery, green pepper, green onions, garlic, mustard, horseradish, oil, vinegar, catsup, Worcestershire sauce and seasonings in a blender container. Process until well mixed. Pour into a large glass serving bowl. Stir in the shrimp. Serve with corn chips. Yield: 32 servings.

Denise Hymel, Gramercy

Seafood Cocktail Spread

2 envelopes unflavored gelatin
3 tablespoons water
1 (10-ounce) can cream of celery soup
1 cup low-fat mayonnaise
8 ounces cream cheese, softened
1 teaspoon onion juice
14 ounces flaked cooked crab meat
14 ounces cooked shrimp, chopped

Soften the gelatin in the water in a saucepan. Stir in the soup. Bring to a boil, stirring until the gelatin dissolves. Remove from the heat and cool completely. Combine the mayonnaise and cream cheese in a bowl and mix well. Stir in the onion juice, crab meat and shrimp. Add to the cooled soup mixture and mix well. Spoon into a 2-quart mold sprayed with nonstick vegetable spray. Chill until firm. Unmold onto a serving plate. Serve with crackers or carrot and celery sticks. Yield: 20 servings.

Constance Bieber, Branch

Shrimp Spread

8 ounces cream cheese, softened
1/2 cup sour cream
1/4 cup mayonnaise
1 cup seafood cocktail sauce
2 cups shredded mozzarella cheese
1 pound peeled cooked shrimp
3 green onions, sliced
3/4 cup finely chopped tomato

Combine the cream cheese, sour cream and mayonnaise in a bowl and beat until smooth. Spread on a 12-inch round serving platter. Layer the cocktail sauce, cheese, shrimp, green onions and tomato over the cream cheese mixture. Chill, covered, until serving time. Serve with chips. Yield: 12 servings.

Becky Creel, Franklinton

Taco Dip

2 envelopes taco seasoning mix
2 (16-ounce) cans refried beans
Red pepper to taste
4 cups sour cream
16 ounces avocado dip
2 cups shredded lettuce
1 cup shredded Cheddar cheese
1 cup chopped tomatoes
1 (7-ounce) jar black olives, drained
1/2 cup chopped green onions

Combine 1 envelope taco seasoning mix, refried beans and red pepper in a bowl and mix well. Combine the remaining envelope of taco seasoning mix and the sour cream in a bowl and mix well. Layer the bean mixture, avocado dip, sour cream mixture, lettuce, cheese, tomatoes, olives and green onions in a large serving bowl. Yield: 40 servings.

Alicia Boudreaux, Lebeau

French Bread and Ham Appetizer

1 envelope ranch-style salad dressing mix
1 cup mayonnaise
1 loaf French bread, split lengthwise
1 cup cubed ham
1 cup chopped green onions
1½ cups shredded Cheddar cheese

Combine the salad dressing mix and mayonnaise in a bowl and mix well. Spread over the cut surfaces of the French bread. Layer the ham, green onions and cheese on the bread. Place on a baking sheet. Bake at 400 degrees for 10 minutes or until the cheese is bubbly. Cut into 2-inch slices. Serve warm. May be frozen before baking. Yield: 20 servings.

Lynn Buzhardt, Zachary

Rice Cakes

2 teaspoons creamy peanut butter
2 miniature apple-cinnamon rice cakes
2 teaspoons chocolate syrup
10 miniature marshmallows

Spread the peanut butter on the rice cakes. Drizzle with the chocolate syrup and top with the marshmallows. These are great for kids' "do-it-yourself snacks." Yield: 1 serving.

Sadie Eastman, Jennings

Sweet Potato Cheese Balls

2 cups mashed cooked sweet potatoes
8 ounces light cream cheese, softened
1½ tablespoons minced jalapeño
1 teaspoon Worcestershire sauce
1 teaspoon Louisiana hot sauce
1 teaspoon seasoned salt
1 teaspoon Panola pepper sauce
¼ cup minced onion
¼ cup finely chopped pecans
1 teaspoon garlic salt
1 teaspoon granulated onion

Combine the sweet potatoes and the cream cheese in a bowl and mix well. Add the jalapeño, Worcestershire sauce, hot sauce, seasoned salt, pepper sauce, onion, pecans, garlic salt and granulated onion. Mix well and shape into balls. Place in a container. Chill, covered, for 8 to 10 hours. Serve with crackers.
Yield: 16 servings.

Kay Haley, Oak Grove

Tortilla Pinwheels

1 cup sour cream
8 ounces cream cheese, softened
1 (4-ounce) can chopped green chiles, drained
1 (4-ounce) can chopped black olives, drained
1 cup shredded Cheddar cheese
1/2 cup chopped green onions
Garlic powder and seasoned salt to taste
5 (10-inch) flour tortillas

Combine the sour cream, cream cheese, chiles, olives, cheese, onions, garlic powder and seasoned salt in a bowl and mix well. Spread the mixture over tortillas. Roll to enclose the filling. Wrap tightly in plastic wrap, twisting the ends to secure. Chill for several hours. Cut into 1/2-to 3/4-inch slices, discarding the ends. Arrange the pinwheels cut side down on a serving plate around a bowl of salsa to serve. Garnish with parsley. Yield: 40 servings.

Donnette W. Bennett, Spearsville

Waldorf Sandwiches

2 cups grated apples
1 tablespoon lemon juice
1 cup finely chopped celery
1 cup chopped walnuts
1/4 cup mayonnaise
1 loaf cinnamon-raisin bread, crusts removed

Combine the apples, lemon juice, celery, walnuts and mayonnaise in a bowl and mix well. Spread on the bread slices. Cut the bread into halves and place on a serving plate. Yield: 20 servings.

Codie Ray, Tallulah

Cinnamon Pecans

1 egg white
1/4 cup sugar
1 teaspoon cinnamon
2 cups pecan halves

Beat the egg white until soft peaks form. Add the sugar and cinnamon gradually, beating until stiff. Fold in the pecans. Spread in a single layer in a greased baking pan. Bake at 300 degrees for 20 minutes. Cool in the pan for 10 minutes and separate the pecan halves. Yield: 8 servings.

Pam Bouillion, Rayne

Eggnog

6 egg yolks
1/2 cup sugar
1 quart milk
6 egg whites
2 tablespoons sugar
1 teaspoon vanilla extract
Nutmeg to taste

Mix the egg yolks and 1/2 cup sugar in a saucepan. Stir in the milk. Cook over medium heat until the mixture coats a spoon, stirring constantly. Pour into a large bowl. Beat the egg whites until soft peaks form. Add 2 tablespoons sugar gradually, beating until stiff. Fold the egg whites, vanilla and nutmeg into the milk mixture. Serve hot or cold. Sprinkle each serving with nutmeg. Yield: 8 servings.

Patricia G. Roussel, Paulina

Easy Punch

1 (64-ounce) can apple juice
1 (64-ounce) can pineapple juice
1 (2-liter) bottle ginger ale, chilled

Combine the apple juice and pineapple juice in a large container and mix well. Freeze, until slushy, stirring frequently. Pour into a punch bowl. Add the cold ginger ale and mix gently. May substitute lemon-lime soda for the ginger ale. Yield: 32 servings.

Phyllis G. Moore, Jonesboro

Yellow Slush Punch

2$^{1}/_{2}$ cups sugar
19 cups lukewarm water
1 (46-ounce) can pineapple juice
1 (12-ounce) can frozen orange juice concentrate
1 (6-ounce) can frozen limeade
1 teaspoon almond extract
1 (1-liter) bottle ginger ale, chilled

Dissolve the sugar in the water in a large freezer container. Add the pineapple juice, orange juice, limeade and almond extract and mix well. Freeze, covered, until needed. Let stand until slushy. Combine with the ginger ale in a punch bowl and mix gently. Yield: 50 servings.

Pam Little, Bastrop

Spiced Tea

6 cups boiling water
6 regular tea bags
1 quart water
15 whole cloves
3 cinnamon sticks
2 cups sugar
1 cup lemon juice
1 (12-ounce) can frozen orange juice, prepared
1 (46-ounce) can pineapple juice
1 (3-ounce) package cherry gelatin

Pour the boiling water over the tea bags in a bowl and allow to steep. Combine 1 quart water, cloves and cinnamon sticks in a large saucepan and bring to a boil over high heat. Reduce the heat. Simmer over low heat for 20 minutes, stirring occasionally. Remove the tea bags and add the tea, sugar, lemon juice, orange juice and pineapple juice to the saucepan. Bring to a boil. Add the gelatin. Cook until the sugar and gelatin dissolve, stirring constantly. Remove the cloves and cinnamon sticks. Serve immediately or store in the refrigerator. Yield: 25 servings.

Billie Middleton, Baton Rouge

Gumbos & Greens

Soups & Salads

Atop of rolling hill in Many, Louisiana, in Sabine Parish, sits the barn of Margaret Martinez's great-great-grandfather. Built in 1850, the barn was used by Margaret's father and is still in use today.

Photograph by Margaret Martinez, Prairieville, LA

Soups & Salads

Cauliflower Soup, 29
Corn Chowder, 30
Crawfish and Corn Chowder, 31
Shrimp and Corn Soup, 32
Shrimp and Corn Fest Chowder, 33
Creole Gumbo, 34
Lumberjack Soup, 35
Mirliton and Shrimp Soup, 36
Taco Soup, 37
Turkey and Sausage Gumbo, 38
Blueberry Salad, 39
Congealed Fruit Delight, 40
Fruit Salad, 41
Fruity Salad, 42
Sour Cream Fruit Salad, 42
Strawberry and Banana Salad, 43
Strawberry Pretzel Salad, 44
Rice and Cranberry Fluff, 45
Harvest Rice Salad, 46
Crawfish Pasta Salad, 47
Super Chicken Salad, 48
Wilted Lettuce Salad, 49
Grandma's Potato Salad, 50
Spinach Salad, 51
Marinated Vegetables, 52
Thousand Island Dressing, 52

Cauliflower Soup

1 head cauliflower
2 tablespoons butter
3 tablespoons finely chopped onion
2 tablespoons flour
1½ cups milk
1½ cups half-and-half
8 ounces Velveeta cheese, cubed
Salt and pepper to taste
1 (15-ounce) can chicken broth

Break the cauliflower into florets, discarding the core. Boil in water to cover in a saucepan until tender. Drain and mash the cauliflower, leaving some chunks. Melt the butter in a large saucepan. Sauté the onion in the butter until tender. Stir in the flour. Add the milk, half-and-half and cheese. Cook for several minutes or until thickened, stirring constantly. Stir in the cauliflower and salt and pepper. Add the chicken broth. Cook until heated through. Yield: 6 servings.

Connie Monroe, Baton Rouge

Corn Chowder

3 slices bacon, chopped
1/2 cup chopped onion
3 tablespoons flour
1 1/2 teaspoons salt
1/8 teaspoon pepper
2 1/2 to 3 cups milk
2 (10-ounce) cans whole kernel corn, drained
1 (17-ounce) can cream-style corn

Fry the bacon in a large saucepan until crisp. Remove the bacon and drain the pan, reserving 3 tablespoons drippings. Sauté the onion in the reserved drippings until tender. Stir in the flour, salt and pepper. Stir in the milk gradually, mixing well after each addition. Add the corn. Cook over medium heat until the soup comes to a boil and is slightly thickened, stirring constantly. Ladle into soup bowls. Sprinkle with the crumbled bacon to serve.
Yield: 6 servings.

Onietta Loewer, Branch

Crawfish and Corn Chowder

1 cup chopped onion
1 cup chopped green bell pepper
1 tablespoon crushed garlic
6 tablespoons margarine
3/4 cup water
1 (10-ounce) can tomatoes with green chiles
1 pound peeled crawfish
2 (16-ounce) cans whole kernel corn
1 (16-ounce) can cream-style corn
Tabasco sauce to taste
Salt and pepper to taste

Sauté the onion, green pepper and garlic in the margarine in a large saucepan over medium heat until tender. Add the water and tomatoes, mashing the tomatoes. Cook for 5 minutes. Add the crawfish, corn, Tabasco sauce, salt and pepper. Simmer for 15 minutes. Yield: 4 servings.

Sheri DeRouen, Jeanerette

Shrimp and Corn Soup

3 tablespoons flour
1/3 cup bacon drippings
2 medium onions, finely chopped
1 large green bell pepper, coarsely chopped
1 rib celery, coarsely chopped
1 clove of garlic, minced
2 pounds medium shrimp, peeled
2 tablespoons finely chopped parsley
1/8 teaspoon sugar
Salt and pepper to taste
1 (28-ounce) can whole peeled tomatoes
1 (10-ounce) can chopped tomatoes with green chiles
1 (16-ounce) can whole kernel corn, drained
1 (11-ounce) can Shoe Peg corn, drained
2 cups water

Stir the flour into the bacon drippings in a large heavy saucepan. Cook over medium heat until golden brown, stirring constantly. Add the onions, green pepper, celery and garlic. Cook for 10 to 15 minutes or until the vegetables are tender. Stir in the shrimp, parsley, sugar, salt and pepper. Simmer for 5 to 10 minutes. Add the undrained whole tomatoes, chopped tomatoes, corn and water. Simmer for 1 hour, adding additional water as needed. Yield: 12 servings.

Beryl Eisworth, St. Francisville

Shrimp and Corn Fest Chowder

12 ounces sliced bacon
2 onions, chopped
3 cloves of garlic, minced
1 cup finely chopped celery
3 tablespoons finely chopped green bell pepper
1/4 cup chopped jalapeños
1 cup finely chopped carrots
1/4 cup flour
8 cups chicken broth
1 (17-ounce) can cream-style corn
2 (16-ounce) cans whole kernel corn
3 cups uncooked rice
1 bay leaf
2 teaspoons salt
1/2 teaspoon pepper
1/8 teaspoon cayenne
1/8 teaspoon paprika
1/2 cup finely chopped potatoes
2 cups half-and-half
1 1/2 pounds shrimp, cooked, peeled, deveined

Cook the bacon in a heavy saucepan over medium heat until crisp. Drain, reserving the drippings. Crumble the bacon and set aside. Sauté the onions, garlic, celery, green pepper, jalapeños and carrots in the bacon drippings for 10 minutes or until tender. Add the flour; mix well. Cook for 2 minutes, stirring constantly. Add the broth, undrained corn and rice. Cook until thickened, stirring occasionally. Add the bay leaf, salt, pepper, cayenne, paprika and potatoes. Cook for 20 minutes or until the potatoes are tender. Stir in the half-and-half. Add the shrimp. Cook until heated through but do not boil. Remove the bay leaf. Ladle into soup bowls. Sprinkle with the bacon and garnish with chopped parsley. Yield: 20 servings.

Leonard J. Hensgens, Crowley

Creole Gumbo

1/2 cup chopped onion
1/4 cup chopped celery
1/4 cup vegetable oil
3 cups water
1 (16-ounce) can stewed tomatoes
1 bay leaf
1 to 1 1/2 teaspoons salt
1 pound peeled medium shrimp
1 (10-ounce) package frozen cut okra
1 teaspoon gumbo filé

Sauté the onion and celery in the oil in a large stockpot over medium-high heat until the onion is lightly browned. Add the water, tomatoes, bay leaf and salt. Simmer, uncovered, for 10 minutes. Stir in the shrimp and okra. Bring to a boil and reduce the heat to medium. Cook, covered, for 10 minutes, stirring occasionally. Stir in the gumbo filé. Simmer, covered, for 5 minutes. Remove the bay leaf. Serve over cooked rice. Yield: 6 servings.

Patty Champlin, Loranger

Lumberjack Soup

1 (10-ounce) can cannellini beans
1 (16-ounce) can mixed vegetables
1 (14-ounce) can beef broth
1 (10-ounce) can tomato soup
1 soup can water
8 to 16 ounces link sausage, cooked, sliced
1 tablespoon parsley flakes
1/4 teaspoon garlic powder
1/2 teaspoon Italian seasoning
1/4 teaspoon pepper
1/2 cup dry red wine
6 slices French bread
1/2 cup shredded mozzarella or Swiss cheese

Combine the beans, undrained vegetables, broth, soup, water, sausage, parsley, garlic, seasoning, pepper and wine in a large saucepan. Simmer for 15 minutes. Ladle into individual ovenproof bowls. Place a slice of bread on each serving. Sprinkle with the cheese. Broil for 4 to 5 minutes or until the cheese melts. May vary the amount of sausage, but do not use hot sausage since the soup is already spicy. Yield: 6 servings.

Anita Schilling, Franklinton

Mirliton and Shrimp Soup

2 pounds unpeeled shrimp
6 cups water
8 large mirlitons (alligator pears)
1 large onion, chopped
2 bunches green onions, chopped
1 rib celery, chopped
1 green bell pepper, chopped
1/2 cup margarine
1/4 cup flour
2 tablespoons finely chopped parsley
Salt and pepper to taste
1 cup evaporated skim milk

Peel the shrimp, discarding the heads and reserving the shells. Bring the water to a boil in a large stockpot and add the shells. Boil for 30 minutes or until the stock is reduced to 4 cups. Strain the stock through a sieve and reserve. Parboil the mirlitons. Peel and cut into cubes. Sauté the onion, green onions, celery and green pepper in the margarine in a large stockpot until tender. Add the flour and mix well. Add the reserved stock. Simmer for 10 minutes. Add the shrimp, mirlitons, parsley, salt and pepper. Simmer for 30 minutes. Add the evaporated milk. Cook until heated through but do not boil. Yield: 6 servings.

Joan Falgoust, St. James

Taco Soup

2 pounds ground beef
1 onion, chopped
2 (15-ounce) cans pinto beans
2 (14-ounce) cans stewed tomatoes
1 (10-ounce) can tomatoes with green chiles
1 (16-ounce) can whole kernel corn
1 envelope taco seasoning
1 envelope ranch-style dressing mix

Brown the ground beef with the onion in a large saucepan, stirring until the ground beef is crumbly; drain. Add the beans, tomatoes and corn. Stir in the taco seasoning and salad dressing mix. Simmer, covered, for 30 to 45 minutes or until the vegetables are tender. Serve with shredded Monterey Jack cheese and corn chips. Yield: 12 servings.

Jann Logan, Gilliam

Turkey and Sausage Gumbo

Carcass of 1 roasted turkey
1 cup flour
1 cup vegetable oil
6 large onions, chopped
5 ribs celery, chopped
1 large green bell pepper, chopped
8 cloves of garlic, chopped
1 (28-ounce) can tomatoes, chopped
4 bay leaves
2 teaspoons thyme
Salt and pepper to taste
1 1/2 pounds andouille sausage, sliced

Combine the turkey carcass with water to cover in a saucepan. Simmer until the meat is loosened from the bones. Remove the turkey from the stock and cool. Remove the meat and discard the bones. Whisk the flour and oil together in a large saucepan. Cook until the roux is dark brown, stirring constantly. Stir in the onions, celery, green pepper, garlic, tomatoes, bay leaves, thyme, roux and salt and pepper. Bring to a boil. Simmer, covered, for 2 hours. Add the sausage. Cook for 1 hour. Degrease the gumbo if needed. Adjust seasonings to taste. Serve with filé.
Yield: 24 servings.

Sherry Harris, Folsom

Blueberry Salad

2 (3-ounce) packages grape gelatin
2 cups boiling water
1 (20-ounce) can crushed pineapple
1 (21-ounce) can blueberry pie filling
8 ounces cream cheese, softened
1/2 cup sugar
1 cup sour cream
1/2 cup chopped pecans
1 teaspoon vanilla extract

Dissolve the gelatin in the boiling water in a bowl. Stir in the undrained pineapple and pie filling. Spoon into a 9x13-inch dish. Chill for 1 hour or until set. Beat the cream cheese and sugar in a mixer bowl until fluffy. Add the sour cream, pecans and vanilla. Spread over the congealed layer. Chill until serving time.
Yield: 8 servings

Joanne Bolding, Oak Grove

Congealed Fruit Delight

2 (3-ounce) packages red mixed fruit gelatin
2 (4-ounce) packages banana cream pudding and pie filling mix
8 ounces cream cheese, softened
1 cup confectioners' sugar
10 ounces whipped topping
1/2 cup chopped walnuts or pecans
2 bananas, sliced

Prepare the gelatin using package directions. Pour into a 9x13-inch dish. Chill until set. Prepare the pudding mix using package directions. Let stand until cool. Beat the cream cheese in a mixer bowl, adding the confectioners' sugar gradually. Stir in 1 cup of the whipped topping. Spread over the gelatin mixture. Sprinkle with the walnuts. Layer the pudding, remaining whipped topping and sliced bananas over the top. Garnish with whole walnuts or pecans. Chill until serving time. May omit nuts if preferred. Yield: 15 servings.

Patty Starkey, Dodson

Fruit Salad

1 (15-ounce) can pineapple chunks
1 (16-ounce) can mandarin oranges
1 (4-ounce) package vanilla pudding and pie filling mix
1 (29-ounce) can pear halves
1 (29-ounce) can peach halves
1/2 (10-ounce) jar maraschino cherries
1/2 cup chopped pecans
1 banana, sliced

Drain the juice from the pineapple and oranges into a medium saucepan, reserving the fruit in a large bowl. Whisk the pudding mix into the juice mixture. Cook over medium heat until the mixture thickens and becomes glossy, stirring constantly. Remove from the heat and cool. Chop the pears, peaches and cherries and add to the reserved fruit. Stir in the pecans and banana. Fold in the pudding mixture. Chill until serving time. Yield: 10 servings.

Margaret Sorenson, Denham Springs

Fruity Salad

12 ounces cottage cheese
1 (3-ounce) package orange gelatin
1 (8-ounce) can mandarin oranges, drained
1 (16-ounce) can crushed pineapple, drained
1 cup chopped pecans
8 ounces whipped topping

Mix the cottage cheese and gelatin in a large bowl. Add the oranges, pineapple and pecans. Fold in the whipped topping. Chill for 2 hours. Yield: 8 servings.

Dean N. Johnson, Jena

Sour Cream Fruit Salad

12 ounces cream cheese, softened
1 cup sour cream
1 (16-ounce) can fruit cocktail
16 ounces miniature marshmallows
1 (8-ounce) jar red maraschino cherries, drained
1/2 cup ground pecans

Beat the cream cheese and the sour cream in a mixer bowl. Stir in the fruit cocktail. Fold in the marshmallows. Spoon into a 9x13-inch dish. Arrange the cherries over the top and sprinkle with the ground pecans. Chill for 3 to 4 hours before serving. Yield: 12 servings.

Martha Scanlan, Church Point

Strawberry and Banana Salad

1 (6-ounce) package strawberry gelatin
1 cup boiling water
4 bananas, mashed
1 (20-ounce) can crushed pineapple
1 (16-ounce) package frozen strawberries, thawed
1 cup sour cream

Dissolve the gelatin in the boiling water in a bowl. Add the bananas, pineapple and strawberries. Chill until the mixture begins to thicken. Spoon half the gelatin into a serving dish. Spread the sour cream carefully over the top. Spoon the remaining gelatin over the sour cream. Chill until firm. Yield: 10 servings.

H.C. Zaunbrecher, Eunice

Strawberry Pretzel Salad

1/4 cup sugar
1 1/2 cups chopped pretzels
1/2 cup melted margarine
8 ounces whipped topping
8 ounces cream cheese, softened
1 cup sugar
1 (6-ounce) package strawberry gelatin
1 1/4 cups boiling water
4 cups frozen strawberries, crushed in blender

Combine the sugar and pretzels in a small bowl. Stir in the margarine. Pat onto the bottom of a 9x13-inch baking dish. Bake at 350 degrees for 10 minutes. Let stand until cool. Mix the whipped topping, cream cheese and sugar in a mixer bowl. Spread over the cooled crust. Dissolve the gelatin in the boiling water in a bowl. Add the crushed strawberries. Pour carefully over the cream cheese layer. Chill until serving time. Yield: 20 servings.

Mary Vail, Lake Charles

Rice and Cranberry Fluff

3 cups cooked white rice
1 (16-ounce) can whole cranberry sauce
1/4 cup sugar
1 (16-ounce) can pineapple tidbits, drained
12 ounces whipped topping
1 1/2 cups chopped pecans

Mix the rice, cranberry sauce, sugar, pineapple, 1/3 of the whipped topping and 1/2 cup of the pecans in a large bowl. Layer the rice mixture, remaining whipped topping and remaining pecans 1/2 at a time in a 4-quart dish. Chill until serving time. Yield: 12 servings.

Joanne Bolding, Oak Grove

Harvest Rice Salad

1½ cups uncooked rice
3 chicken bouillon cubes
¼ cup vegetable oil
2 tablespoons vinegar
1½ teaspoons salt
⅛ teaspoon pepper
1 cup black olives, sliced
2 hard-cooked eggs, chopped
1½ cups chopped dill pickles
1 cup chopped onion
½ cup mayonnaise
2 tablespoons mustard

Cook the rice using the package directions and adding the bouillon cubes. Blend the oil, vinegar, salt and pepper with a whisk in a small bowl. Pour over the hot rice in a large bowl, tossing to mix. Let stand until cool. Stir in the olives, eggs, pickles, onion, mayonnaise and mustard, tossing to mix. Chill until serving time. Yield: 10 servings.

Lacey Hetzel, Jennings

Crawfish Pasta Salad

16 ounces small macaroni
1 pound cleaned crawfish tails
4 hard-cooked eggs, chopped
1 finely chopped green bell pepper
1 finely chopped tomato
1/4 teaspoon salt
1/2 teaspoon pepper
1 1/2 tablespoons sweet pickle relish
2 teaspoons Worcestershire sauce
2 teaspoons Tabasco sauce
3/4 cup mayonnaise

Cook the macaroni using the package directions. Rinse in cold water and drain. Combine the crawfish tails, eggs, green pepper, tomato, salt, pepper, pickle relish, Worcestershire sauce, Tabasco sauce and mayonnaise in a large bowl. Stir in the macaroni. Chill, covered, for 8 to 12 hours. Stir to mix before serving. Yield: 6 servings.

Norma J. Miller, Eunice

Super Chicken Salad

3/4 cup chopped green onions
1/2 cup chopped green bell pepper
1/2 cup chopped celery
1/2 head lettuce, torn
4 cups chopped cooked chicken
1 (16-ounce) can green peas, drained
1 (8-ounce) can sliced water chestnuts, drained
1 (16-ounce) can sliced beets, drained
1 cup mayonnaise
2 to 3 tablespoons sugar

Combine the green onions, green pepper and celery in a small bowl. Layer the lettuce, chicken, green onions mixture, peas, water chestnuts and beets in a 9x13-inch dish. Spread the mayonnaise over the beets, sealing to the edge. Sprinkle with the sugar. Chill for 8 to 12 hours. Garnish with shredded Cheddar cheese, sliced hard-cooked eggs and crumbled bacon. Yield: 8 servings.

Angie B. Futch, Farmerville

Wilted Lettuce Salad

2 cups torn lettuce
4 slices bacon
3 tablespoons sugar
1/4 cup vinegar

Rinse and drain the lettuce. Place in salad bowls and set aside. Fry the bacon in a saucepan until crisp. Remove the bacon and drain, reserving the drippings. Add the sugar and vinegar to the drippings. Simmer for 1 minute. Stir in the crumbled bacon. Pour over the lettuce and serve immediately. Yield: 2 servings.

Margaret Brewster, Dubach

Grandma's Potato Salad

8 large red potatoes
8 eggs
3/4 cup white vinegar
1/4 cup water
1 cup sugar
1 onion, grated
2 teaspoons salt
1 teaspoon pepper
5 tablespoons mayonnaise
1 tablespoon mustard
1/2 cup melted margarine
5 hard-cooked eggs, mashed

Boil the potatoes in water to cover in a large saucepan until tender; drain and cool. Peel and chop the potatoes and set aside. Whisk the eggs, vinegar and water in a saucepan. Cook until thickened, stirring constantly. Let stand until cool. Mix the sugar, onion, salt, pepper, mayonnaise, mustard and margarine in a bowl. Stir in the mashed eggs. Pour over the potatoes in a large bowl. Stir in the vinegar mixture. Chill until serving time. Yield: 25 servings.

Betty Jo Brian, Zachary

Spinach Salad

6 slices bacon
1 egg
1/2 cup sugar
1/2 cup white vinegar
3/4 teaspoon salt
10 ounces fresh spinach or leaf lettuce
6 green onions, chopped
2 (11-ounce) cans mandarin oranges, drained
1/2 cup slivered almonds, toasted

Fry the bacon in a skillet. Drain and crumble the bacon, reserving 1 1/2 teaspoons drippings. Beat the egg in a small saucepan. Add the sugar, vinegar, salt and reserved drippings. Cook until thickened, stirring constantly. Chill until serving time. Rinse and drain the spinach; remove and discard the stems. Combine with the green onions, oranges, crumbled bacon and almonds in a large bowl. Add the dressing and toss to coat well. Serve immediately. Yield: 8 servings.

Billie Middleton, Baton Rouge

Marinated Vegetables

1 (16-ounce) can green beans, drained
1 (16-ounce) can Shoe Peg corn, drained
1 (16-ounce) can green peas, drained
1 cup chopped green bell pepper
1 cup chopped onion
1 cup chopped celery
1 (2-ounce) jar pimento
1/2 cup vinegar
1/2 cup vegetable oil
1 cup sugar
1/2 teaspoon salt
1 teaspoon pepper

Combine the beans, corn, peas, green pepper, onion, celery and pimento in a large bowl. Mix the vinegar, oil, sugar, salt and pepper in a saucepan. Bring to a boil. Let stand until cool. Pour over the vegetables. Chill for 24 hours to enhance the flavor. Yield: 6 servings.

Carolyn Walker, Ruston

Thousand Island Dressing

2 large dill pickles
2 hard-cooked eggs
1 large onion
2 cups mayonnaise
1/4 cup (or more) catsup

Chop the pickles, eggs and onion. Combine with the mayonnaise in a large bowl. Add the catsup. Chill until serving time. Yield: 15 servings.

Lois Dodson, Shreveport

Delta Delights

Meat, Game & Poultry

Aptly named for its unique shape, this 500-year-old cypress remnant, known to the locals as "The Cathedral," is a focal point of the Atchafalaya Basin. The world's largest hardwood swamp is filled with such natural wonders, carved by time, wind and weather.

Photograph by Judy Jacobs, Baton Rouge, LA

Meats, Game & Poultry

Barbecue Beef Sandwiches, 55
Beef Strips with Angel Hair Pasta, 56
Beefy Fettuccini, 57
Burger Cheese Casserole, 58
Beef and Cheese Pie, 59
Coal Miner's Pie, 60
Enchiladas Acapulco, 61
Fiesta Beef and Rice, 62
Real Italian Lasagna, 63
Beef Lasagna, 64
Meat and Potato Casserole, 65
Beefy Oyster Dressing, 66
Wagon Wheel Loaf, 67
Best Barbecue Sauce, 68
Creole Pork Chops, 69
Pork Chop and Rice Bake, 70
Black-Eyed Pea Jambalaya, 70
Easy Oven Jambalaya, 71
Rice-Cooker Jambalaya, 72
Sausage Jambalaya, 73
Breakfast Casserole, 74
Sunday Eggs, 75
Slow-Cooker Teriyaki Venison, 76
Deer Tenderloin, 77
Venison Meat Pies, 78
Venison Patties over Fettuccini, 79
Wild Beast Feast, 80
Grilled Dove, 81
Delicious Duck, 82
Chicken Broccoli Cups, 83
Chicken Casserole, 84
Cheesy Chicken Casserole, 85
Chicken Creole, 86
Chicken Divan, 87
Mexican Chicken, 88
Onion and Cheese Chicken, 89
Chicken and Rice Casserole, 90
Chicken Spaghetti, 91
Chicken in Tomato Gravy, 92
Easy Chicken Stew, 93
Chicken Casserole with White Beans and Rice, 93
Chicken and Dumplings, 94

Barbecue Beef Sandwiches

1 (3-pound) boneless chuck roast
1 medium onion, chopped
1/2 cup chopped celery
1 1/2 cups catsup
1/4 cup packed brown sugar
1/4 cup vinegar
2 tablespoons dry mustard
2 teaspoons Worcestershire sauce
2 teaspoons salt
1 teaspoon chili powder
1/2 teaspoon paprika
1/2 teaspoon garlic salt
Hot pepper sauce to taste

Place the chuck roast, onion, celery and enough water to cover in a 3-quart saucepan. Bring to a boil and reduce the heat. Simmer for 2 1/2 to 3 hours. Strain the broth, reserving 2 cups. Shred the meat and return to the saucepan. Mix the reserved broth with the catsup, brown sugar, vinegar, dry mustard, Worcestershire sauce and seasonings in a small bowl. Add to the saucepan. Simmer, covered, for 1 hour, stirring occasionally. Serve on buns if desired. Yield: 15 servings.

Linda Williams, Keithville

Beef Strips with Angel Hair Pasta

1 large purple onion, sliced
2 pounds beef sirloin, thinly sliced
2 tablespoons canola or olive oil
8 ounces mushrooms, sliced
2 yellow squash, sliced
2 zucchini, sliced
1 (16-ounce) can chunky-style tomatoes
Salt and pepper to taste
1 (16-ounce) package angel hair pasta, cooked

Sauté the onion and beef in the oil in a large skillet until the beef is slightly pink. Add the mushrooms, yellow squash and zucchini. Sauté until the vegetables are tender-crisp. Stir in the tomatoes. Cook until heated through. Season with salt and pepper. Serve over the angel hair pasta. Yield: 8 servings.

Lola Griffin, Abbeville

Beefy Fettuccini

1½ pounds ground beef
1 onion, chopped
1 rib celery, chopped
1 green bell pepper, chopped
1 bunch green onions, chopped
1 clove of garlic, minced
½ cup melted margarine
1 tablespoon flour
1 (5-ounce) can evaporated milk
8 ounces jalapeño cheese, chopped or cubed
1 (10-ounce) can tomatoes with green chiles
Cajun seasoning to taste
1 (8-ounce) package fettuccini

Brown the ground beef in a skillet, stirring until crumbly; drain and set aside. Sauté the onion, celery, green pepper, green onions and garlic in the margarine in the skillet until tender. Stir in the browned beef and flour. Simmer for 15 minutes. Stir in the evaporated milk and half the cheese. Add the tomatoes and Cajun seasoning. Simmer for 15 minutes. Cook the fettuccini using the package directions; drain. Stir into the beef mixture. Place in a greased 9x13-inch baking dish and top with the remaining cheese. Bake at 350 degrees for 15 minutes or until the cheese melts.
Yield: 6 servings.

Janell DeRouen, Jeanerette

Burger Cheese Casserole

2 pounds lean ground beef
1 teaspoon seasoned salt
1 teaspoon lemon pepper
1 tablespoon Worcestershire sauce
1 (10-ounce) can cream of mushroom soup
1 (10-ounce) can cream of onion soup
1 (10-ounce) can cream of celery soup
16 ounces cream cheese, softened
1/2 cup bread crumbs

Brown the ground beef with the seasoned salt, lemon pepper and Worcestershire sauce in a skillet, stirring until the ground beef is crumbly; drain. Mix the soups and cream cheese in a bowl. Add half the soup mixture to the ground beef. Place in a 9x13-inch baking dish. Top with the remaining soup mixture. Sprinkle with the bread crumbs. Bake at 350 degrees for 20 minutes. May drizzle 1/4 cup melted butter over the bread crumbs before baking. May pour hot water over the ground beef when draining in a colander and use low-fat soups and cream cheese to reduce fat content. Yield: 8 servings.

Codie Ray, Tallulah

Beef and Cheese Pie

1 pound ground beef
1 cup chopped onion
1/2 teaspoon salt
1 cup shredded Cheddar cheese
1 cup milk
1/2 cup baking mix
2 eggs

Brown the ground beef and onion in a skillet, stirring until the ground beef is crumbly; drain. Add the salt. Place in a greased 9-inch pie plate. Sprinkle with the cheese. Blend the milk, baking mix and eggs in a bowl. Pour over the beef mixture. Bake at 400 degrees for 25 minutes. May top with 1/2 cup salsa before serving. Yield: 6 servings.

Jackie Brown, Jennings

Coal Miner's Pie

1 pound ground beef
2 medium onions, chopped
2 green bell peppers, chopped
1 (15-ounce) can tomato sauce
2 cups canned whole kernel corn
2 tablespoons chili powder
1 1/4 teaspoons salt
1 (8 1/2-ounce) package corn bread mix

Brown the ground beef with the onions in a skillet, stirring until the ground beef is crumbly; drain. Stir in the green peppers, tomato sauce, corn, chili powder and salt. Simmer for 15 minutes. Pour into a 8x8-inch baking dish. Prepare the corn bread mix using the package directions. Spread over the pie. Bake at 350 degrees until the corn bread is golden brown. May freeze casserole if desired. Yield: 6 servings.

Betty Sue Miller, Mount Hermon

Enchiladas Acapulco

1 pound ground beef
1 (8-ounce) can tomato sauce
3/4 cup chopped green bell peppers
1 (8-ounce) can kidney beans, drained
8 ounces process cheese, cubed
Oil for frying
8 (6-inch) flour tortillas
1/2 cup chopped tomatoes

Brown the ground beef in a skillet, stirring until the ground beef is crumbly; drain. Add the tomato sauce and 1/2 cup of the green peppers. Simmer over medium heat for 5 minutes, stirring occasionally. Add the kidney beans and half the cheese. Cook until the cheese melts. Heat the oil in a small skillet. Fry the tortillas in the oil just until softened; drain. Fill each tortilla with 1/4 cup beef mixture, roll up and place seam side down in a 7x11-inch baking dish. Bake, covered, at 350 degrees for 20 minutes. Top with the remaining cheese. Bake, uncovered, for 5 to 8 minutes or until the cheese melts. Top with the remaining green peppers and tomatoes. Yield: 4 servings.

Edda Hoffpauir, Lake Charles

Fiesta Beef and Rice

1 pound ground beef
1/2 cup chopped onion
1 cup mild salsa
1 cup uncooked rice
2 cups water
1 (16-ounce) package frozen vegetable mix
1 teaspoon salt
1 teaspoon pepper
1/2 teaspoon garlic powder
4 ounces Cheddar cheese, shredded

Brown the ground beef with the onion in a skillet, stirring until the ground beef is crumbly; drain. Add the salsa, rice, water, frozen vegetables, salt, pepper and garlic powder. Simmer, covered, over low heat for 30 minutes or until the rice and vegetables are tender. Top with the cheese. Cover and let stand until the cheese melts. Yield: 4 servings.

Melissa Brown, Jennings

Real Italian Lasagna

2 pounds ground beef
2 or 3 onions, chopped
1 (28-ounce) can whole tomatoes
1 (8-ounce) can tomato sauce
1/4 teaspoon sage
1/4 teaspoon parsley flakes
1/4 teaspoon rosemary
1/4 teaspoon thyme
1/4 teaspoon oregano
1/4 teaspoon celery salt
1/4 teaspoon garlic powder
1/4 teaspoon marjoram
1/4 teaspoon dry mustard
1/4 teaspoon Worcestershire sauce
Salt and pepper to taste
6 to 8 lasagna noodles, cooked
8 ounces cottage cheese or ricotta cheese
10 ounces Cheddar cheese, shredded
10 ounces mozzarella cheese, shredded
1 cup grated Parmesan cheese

Brown the ground beef in a skillet, stirring until crumbly; drain. Add the onions, tomatoes, tomato sauce and seasonings. Simmer for 30 minutes or longer, adding water gradually as needed. Layer the lasagna noodles, sauce, cottage cheese, Cheddar, mozzarella and Parmesan cheeses 1/2 at a time in a greased 9x13-inch baking dish. Bake at 350 degrees for 25 minutes. Yield: 8 servings.

Henrietta Landry, Elton

Beef Lasagna

2 pounds ground beef
1 medium onion, chopped
1 clove of garlic, chopped
1 (16-ounce) can tomato sauce
2 (8-ounce) cans pizza sauce
1 teaspoon salt
1 teaspoon oregano
1/2 teaspoon basil
1/2 cup grated Parmesan cheese
1 (8-ounce) package lasagna noodles, cooked
1 cup small curd cottage cheese
8 ounces mozzarella cheese, shredded

Brown the ground beef with the onion and garlic in a skillet, stirring until the ground beef is crumbly; drain. Add the tomato sauce, pizza sauce, salt, oregano and basil. Cook, covered, over low heat for 20 minutes. Set aside 1 cup meat sauce and 1/4 cup Parmesan cheese for the topping. Spoon 1 cup of remaining meat sauce into the bottom of a greased 9x13-inch baking dish. Layer the lasagna noodles, remaining meat sauce, cottage cheese, mozzarella cheese and remaining Parmesan cheese 1/2 at a time in the baking dish. Top with the reserved meat sauce and Parmesan cheese. Bake at 350 degrees for 30 minutes. Let stand for 10 minutes before serving. Yield: 10 servings.

Mary Vail, Lake Charles

Meat and Potato Casserole

2 pounds ground chuck
2 large onions, chopped
2 teaspoons salt
2 teaspoons pepper
1 (10-ounce) can tomatoes with green chiles
3 (10-ounce) cans cream of chicken soup
2 soup cans water
8 medium potatoes, baked, peeled
16 slices American cheese

Brown the ground chuck with the onions, salt and pepper in a large skillet, stirring until the ground chuck is crumbly; drain. Stir in the tomatoes, soup and water. Cook over low heat until heated through, stirring occasionally. Slice the potatoes 1/3 inch thick. Layer the meat mixture, potatoes and cheese slices 1/2 at a time in a 10x13-inch baking dish coated with nonstick cooking spray. Bake at 350 degrees for 25 minutes or until the cheese melts. Yield: 8 servings.

Nita Gaines, Quitman

Beefy Oyster Dressing

1 large sweet potato
2 pounds ground beef
1 pound ground pork
2 onions, finely chopped
1/2 clove of garlic, finely chopped
1 dozen oysters
1/2 loaf dry French bread, sliced
Salt and pepper to taste

Bake the sweet potato until tender. Peel and chop into small pieces. Brown the ground beef and ground pork in a skillet, stirring until crumbly. Remove to a bowl with a slotted spoon, reserving the drippings. Sauté the onions and garlic in the drippings until tender; drain. Add the ground beef mixture, sweet potato and undrained oysters to the skillet. Soak the French bread in water, squeeze out the water and add to the skillet. Cook over low heat for 15 minutes or until done to taste. Skim to remove any excess fat. Season with salt and pepper. May chop oysters before adding to skillet if desired. Yield: 8 servings.

Patricia G. Roussel, Paulina

Wagon Wheel Loaf

1¼ cups picante sauce
¼ cup reduced-sodium tomato paste
1¼ pounds extra-lean ground beef
½ cup finely chopped onion
½ cup bread crumbs
1 egg, lightly beaten
¾ teaspoon Italian herb seasoning
1 cup shredded low-sodium low-fat mozzarella cheese
1 (4-ounce) can sliced mushrooms, drained
½ cup chopped green onions
¼ cup sliced black olives

Combine the picante sauce and tomato paste in a small bowl. Combine ½ cup picante sauce mixture with the ground beef, onion, bread crumbs, egg and seasoning in a large bowl. Pat ½ of the beef mixture into an 8-inch circle on waxed paper. Place on a rack in a shallow 8-inch baking pan. Spread with ½ cup of the picante sauce mixture. Sprinkle with ½ cup cheese and top with the mushrooms, green onions and black olives. Pat the remaining beef mixture into an 8-inch circle on wax paper. Place over the filling, pinching the edges to seal. Bake at 350 degrees for 1 hour. Top with the remaining picante sauce mixture and cheese. Bake for 3 minutes longer. Serve with additional picante sauce if desired. The loaf may be sliced for sandwiches or crumbled and used as filling with refrigerator biscuit dough. Bake the biscuits using the package directions. Yield: 6 servings.

Monica Lyons, Church Point

Best Barbecue Sauce

10 large onions, sliced
1 head of garlic, chopped
1 tablespoon pepper
2 cups melted butter
11 (14-ounce) bottles catsup
11 catsup bottles water
5 lemons
6 (10-ounce) bottles Worcestershire sauce
1 teaspoon brown sugar
1 teaspoon (heaping) prepared mustard
1 tablespoon vinegar
1 (2-ounce) bottle Tabasco sauce

Sauté the onions and garlic with the pepper in the butter in a large stockpot until tender. Stir in the catsup and water. Cut the lemons into halves and squeeze out the juice. Add the lemon juice and rinds to the pan. Stir in the Worcestershire sauce, brown sugar, mustard, vinegar and Tabasco sauce. Bring the mixture to a boil and reduce the heat. Simmer, partially covered, for 2 to 3 hours, stirring frequently. Remove the lemon rinds. Use the sauce to baste meat during the last hour of cooking. Freeze the sauce in meal-size portions if desired. Yield: 12 quarts.

Reynold Minsky, Lake Providence

Creole Pork Chops

1 cup flour
Salt, pepper and paprika to taste
6 (4-ounce) center-cut pork chops
2 tablespoons vegetable oil
1 (16-ounce) can tomatoes
1 (8-ounce) can tomato sauce
1 small onion, chopped
1 green bell pepper, chopped
1/2 cup sliced mushrooms
1/4 cup water

Mix the flour and the seasonings. Coat the pork chops with the seasoned flour. Brown the pork chops in the oil in a skillet; drain. Place in a 2-quart baking dish. Add the tomatoes, tomato sauce, onion, green pepper, mushrooms and water. Bake, covered, at 325 degrees for 1 1/2 to 2 hours or until cooked through. Serve with rice. Yield: 6 servings.

Paige Carlisle, Shreveport

Pork Chop and Rice Bake

6 (4-ounce) pork chops
2 tablespoons vegetable oil
1 cup uncooked rice
1 envelope onion soup mix
1 (4-ounce) can sliced mushrooms
2 tablespoons chopped pimento

Brown the pork chops in the oil in a skillet. Spread the rice in a 9x13-inch baking dish. Sprinkle with the soup mix. Drain the mushrooms, reserving the liquid. Layer the mushrooms and pimento over the soup mix. Add enough hot water to the mushroom liquid to make 3 cups. Pour into the baking dish. Arrange the pork chops over the rice. Bake, covered with foil, at 350 degrees for 45 to 60 minutes or until the pork chops are cooked through. Bake, uncovered, for 10 minutes longer or until the excess liquid evaporates. Yield: 6 servings.

Joanne Bolding, Oak Grove

Black-Eyed Pea Jambalaya

1 package jambalaya mix or leftover jambalaya
1 (16-ounce) can black-eyed peas, drained

Prepare the jambalaya mix using the package directions. Stir in the black-eyed peas. Cook until heated through. Serve with biscuits or corn bread muffins and a salad. Yield: 4 servings.

Cherlyon Nesom, Denham Springs

Easy Oven Jambalaya

1 pound smoked sausage, sliced
1 medium onion, chopped
1 (10-ounce) can mushroom steak sauce
1 (10-ounce) can beef consommé
1 teaspoon minced garlic or garlic powder
1 cup water
1/2 cup chopped green onions
1/2 cup chopped green bell pepper
1 cup uncooked rice

Sauté the sausage and onion in a skillet until the onion is tender. Stir in the steak sauce, consommé and garlic. Add the water. Bring the mixture to a boil. Cook for 5 minutes. Add the green onions, green pepper and rice. Bring to a boil for 3 minutes, stirring occasionally. Spoon into a baking dish. Bake at 350 degrees for 20 minutes; stir to mix. Bake for 10 to 15 minutes longer or until heated through. Yield: 6 servings.

Shannon Hymel, Lutcher

Rice-Cooker Jambalaya

1 (16-ounce) can black-eyed peas with jalapeños
1½ cups uncooked rice
1 medium onion, chopped
1 (14-ounce) can beef broth
1 (4-ounce) can mushrooms, drained
½ cup margarine
1 pound smoked sausage, cut into bite-size pieces
Salt and pepper to taste

Combine the black-eyed peas, rice, onion, beef broth, mushrooms, margarine and sausage in a rice cooker. Season to taste. Cook using the rice cooker instructions. May combine all the ingredients in a baking dish. Bake at 350 degrees for 30 to 40 minutes or until the liquid is absorbed. Yield: 6 servings.

Norma J. Miller, Eunice

Sausage Jambalaya

1 pound smoked sausage, cut up
1/2 cup chopped green onions
1 medium green bell pepper, chopped
1 1/4 teaspoons garlic powder
1 pound ground beef
2 (14-ounce) cans stewed tomatoes
1/2 teaspoon salt
1/4 teaspoon pepper
1 cup uncooked rice
1 1/2 cups water

Brown the sausage in a skillet; drain and remove from the skillet. Add the green onions, green pepper, garlic powder and ground beef to the skillet. Cook, stirring until the ground beef is crumbly; drain. Add the sausage, tomatoes, salt and pepper. Simmer, covered, for 20 minutes. Add the rice and water. Cook, covered, for 25 minutes longer or until the rice is tender.
Yield: 6 servings.

Patty Champlin, Loranger

Breakfast Casserole

2 pounds breakfast sausage, sliced
1 (8-ounce) package croutons
2 cups shredded Monterey Jack cheese
6 eggs
1/2 cup milk
Salt and pepper to taste

Brown the sausage in a small skillet; drain. Layer the croutons, sausage and cheese in a greased 9x13-inch baking dish. Beat the eggs, milk and seasonings in a bowl. Pour over the layers. Bake at 400 degrees for 20 minutes or until golden brown. May top with picante sauce if desired. May substitute bacon or ham for the sausage and Cheddar cheese for the Monterey Jack cheese or use other seasonings as desired. Yield: 6 servings.

Henrietta Landry, Elton

Sunday Eggs

6 eggs, beaten
1 (17-ounce) can cream-style corn
2 cups shredded sharp Cheddar cheese
1 (4-ounce) can chopped green chiles
1 teaspoon Worcestershire sauce
1/2 teaspoon black pepper
Salt and Tabasco sauce to taste

Combine the eggs, corn, cheese, green chiles, Worcestershire sauce and seasonings in a large bowl and mix well. Pour into a 2-quart baking dish. Bake at 325 degrees for 1 hour or until firm. May be made up to 24 hours ahead of time and refrigerated until time to bake. Yield: 6 servings.

Ann Dodson, Shreveport

Slow-Cooker Teriyaki Venison

4 (4-ounce) backstrap venison chops
1 to 1½ cups soy sauce
½ teaspoon minced garlic

Marinate the venison in ½ cup soy sauce in a bowl in the refrigerator for 2 hours to overnight. Place the venison in a slow cooker. Stir the garlic into the remaining soy sauce. Pour over the venison. Cook, covered, on Low for 4 hours or until tender. Yield: 4 servings.

Phyllis G. Moore, Jonesboro

Deer Tenderloin

1 pound deer tenderloin
Salt and pepper to taste
1 (12-ounce) can cola
1 cup flour or cracker crumbs
Vegetable oil for frying

Pound the tenderloin with a meat mallet. Season with salt and pepper. Place in a shallow dish. Pour the cola over the tenderloin. Marinate for 30 minutes or longer in the refrigerator. Coat the tenderloin with the flour. Fry the tenderloin in the oil in a skillet until golden brown. Serve with rice, pan gravy and homemade biscuits if desired. Yield: 4 servings.

Tammie Stutts, Pioneer

Venison Meat Pies

1 pound ground venison
8 ounces ground pork
1 bunch green onions, chopped
1 green bell pepper, chopped
3 cloves of garlic, minced
Salt, black pepper and red pepper to taste
1 tablespoon flour
3/4 cup shortening
2 cups flour
1 tablespoon cold water

Sauté the ground venison and pork with the green onions, green pepper, garlic and seasonings in a large skillet coated with cooking spray, stirring until the meats are crumbly but not dry. Stir in 1 tablespoon flour. Remove the skillet from the heat. Cut the shortening into 2 cups flour in a bowl until crumbly. Add the water, mixing with a fork until the mixture forms a ball. Roll out the dough 1/8 inch thick. Cut into 8 rectangles. Place the venison mixture down 1 side of each rectangle. Fold the dough over and crimp the edges to seal. Place on a baking sheet. Bake at 350 degrees for 20 minutes or until golden brown. May also make with prepared pie pastry or crescent rolls. Yield: 8 servings.

Jan Thrash, Ringgold

Venison Patties over Fettuccini

1 pound ground venison
1/2 cup baking mix
1/2 cup tomato juice
1/4 cup chopped green bell pepper
1 egg, beaten
1 clove of garlic, minced
Salt, pepper, Worcestershire sauce and oregano to taste
1 (16-ounce) package fettuccini, cooked

Combine the venison, baking mix, tomato juice, green pepper, egg, garlic and seasonings in a bowl and mix well. Shape into 6 patties. Place in a shallow baking dish coated with nonstick cooking spray. Bake at 400 degrees for 20 minutes. Serve over the fettuccini. Top with Parmesan cheese and sliced stuffed olives if desired. May add a sauce to the fettuccini if desired.
Yield: 6 servings.

Beryl Eisworth, St. Francisville

Wild Beast Feast

6 medium onions, chopped
2 green bell peppers, chopped
1 clove of garlic, finely chopped
2 bunches green onions, chopped
1 cup melted butter
1 pound each venison, duck, rabbit, alligator, andouille sausage, cut into bite-size pieces
4 envelopes jambalaya mix
Salt, black pepper and red pepper to taste
Worcestershire sauce, hot sauce and browning sauce to taste
1 pound crawfish, cut into bite-size pieces

Sauté the onions, green peppers, garlic and green onions in 1/2 cup butter in a heavy ovenproof black iron pot until tender. Remove the vegetables. Brown the venison, duck, rabbit, alligator and andouille in the remaining 1/2 cup butter and the drippings in the pot. Add the sautéed vegetables. Stir in the jambalaya mix and the water called for in the package directions. Add the salt, black pepper, red pepper, Worcestershire sauce, hot sauce and browning sauce. Stir in the crawfish. Bring to a boil. Place in the oven. Bake, covered, at 375 degrees for 35 to 40 minutes or until done to taste. Serve with white beans, salad and garlic bread. May substitute chicken stock for the water called for on the jambalaya mix. May substitute chicken, raccoon, squirrel, venison sausage or wild pork for the meat in this recipe or vary the amounts. May also substitute shrimp or oysters for the crawfish. Yield: 12 servings.

Raymond Taylor, Clinton

Grilled Dove

20 dove breasts
20 slices bacon
1/4 cup honey
1 cup melted butter

Rinse the dove; pat dry. Wrap the dove in the bacon. Mix the honey and butter in a small bowl. Place the dove on a grill over low heat. Grill for 30 to 45 minutes, basting occasionally with the honey mixture. Serve over wild rice. May add mesquite or hickory wood to the grill for a flavor variation. Yield: 10 servings.

Buddy Cook, Shreveport

Delicious Duck

4 whole ducks
2 tablespoons vegetable oil
Salt and pepper to taste
1 (10-ounce) can cream of mushroom soup
1 soup can water
1 envelope dry onion soup mix
10 ounces (or more) water

Rinse the ducks; pat dry. Brown the ducks on all sides in the oil in a heavy cast-iron skillet. Sprinkle with salt and pepper. Mix the soup, water and soup mix in a bowl. Pour over the ducks. Simmer, covered, for 2 to 3 hours or until tender, adding water as needed. Serve with dressing. May substitute one 2- to 3-pound venison roast for the ducks. Serve with mashed potatoes.
Yield: 4 servings.

Maryanna Perryman, Dobberly

Chicken Broccoli Cups

1 (10-count) can (or more) refrigerated biscuits
6 boneless chicken breasts, cooked, chopped
1 (10-ounce) package frozen chopped broccoli, cooked, drained
1 (10-ounce) can cream of mushroom soup
3/4 cup shredded Cheddar cheese

Press the biscuits over bottoms and sides of lightly greased muffin cups. Combine the chicken, broccoli and soup in a bowl and mix well. Spoon into the biscuit-lined muffin cups. Top with the cheese. Bake at 400 degrees for 10 minutes.
Yield: 5 servings.

Nettie Spurgeon, Zachary

Chicken Casserole

1 ($3^1/_2$-pound) stewing chicken, cooked, boned
1 cup chopped celery
1 cup chopped onion
1 (10-ounce) can cream of chicken soup
1 cup mayonnaise
2 tablespoons lemon juice
Salt and pepper to taste
2 cups crushed potato chips

Chop the chicken into bite-size pieces. Combine the chicken, celery, onion, soup, mayonnaise, lemon juice and seasonings in a bowl and mix well. Spoon into a greased 2-quart baking dish. Top with the chips. Bake, uncovered, at 325 degrees for 30 minutes or until bubbly. May be frozen. Yield: 6 servings.

Mrs. Glen Robinson, Jonesboro

Cheesy Chicken Casserole

6 boneless chicken breasts (about 1 1/4 pounds)
1 (16-ounce) package vermicelli
1 (10-ounce) package frozen broccoli
1 medium onion, chopped
1/2 cup chopped celery
1/2 cup chopped green bell pepper
1/2 cup melted margarine
8 ounces mushrooms, sliced
16 ounces Velveeta cheese, cubed
1 (10-ounce) can cream of mushroom soup
1 (10-ounce) can tomatoes with green chiles
1/4 cup grated Parmesan cheese
1/4 cup bread crumbs

Rinse the chicken well. Cook in water to cover in a saucepan until tender. Remove from the broth, cool, and cut into bite-size pieces, reserving the broth. Cook the vermicelli and broccoli in the reserved broth until tender; drain. Sauté the onion, celery and green pepper in the margarine in a large skillet until tender. Add the mushrooms, Velveeta cheese, soup and tomatoes. Cook until the cheese melts, stirring constantly. Fold in the chicken, vermicelli and broccoli. Spoon into a greased 9x13-inch baking dish. Sprinkle with the Parmesan cheese and top with the bread crumbs. Bake, uncovered, at 350 degrees for 30 to 45 minutes or until bubbly. Prepare 1 day in advance for the best results. May freeze leftovers. Yield: 8 servings.

Beverly Zeringue, Vacherie

Chicken Creole

2 pounds boneless chicken
1 onion, chopped
2 green bell peppers, chopped
4 ribs celery, chopped
1 tablespoon vegetable oil
1 (16-ounce) can diced tomatoes
2 (10-ounce) cans tomato soup
1 bay leaf
2 cups water
3 cups cooked rice

Rinse the chicken. Cook as desired; drain and chop. Sauté the onion, green peppers and celery in the oil in a large skillet until tender. Add the tomatoes, soup, bay leaf and water. Simmer for 2 hours. Add the chicken. Cook for 30 minutes longer. Remove the bay leaf. Serve over the rice. Yield: 10 servings.

Pam Holloway, Marion

Chicken Divan

2½ cups cooked rice
2 (10-ounce) packages frozen broccoli spears or chopped broccoli, cooked
5 boneless chicken breasts, cooked, chopped
1 (6-ounce) can mushrooms, drained
1 (10-ounce) can cream of mushroom soup
1 (10-ounce) can cream of chicken soup
½ soup can water
1 cup mayonnaise
1 teaspoon lemon juice
½ teaspoon curry powder
2 tablespoons butter or margarine
½ cup shredded Cheddar cheese
½ cup bread crumbs

Spread the rice in a 9x13-inch baking dish sprayed with nonstick cooking spray. Layer the broccoli, chicken and mushrooms over the rice. Combine the soups, water, mayonnaise, lemon juice and curry powder in a bowl. Pour over the layers. Dot with the butter. Sprinkle with the cheese and bread crumbs. Bake at 350 degrees for 30 minutes. May cover for the first 20 minutes for a less crisp topping. Yield: 8 servings.

Loretta Treme, Elton

Mexican Chicken

2 cups chopped cooked chicken
8 ounces Velveeta cheese, cubed
1 onion, finely chopped
1 (12-ounce) package tortilla chips, crumbled
1 (10-ounce) can tomatoes with green chiles
1 (10-ounce) can cream of mushroom soup
1 (10-ounce) can cream of chicken soup

Layer the chicken, cheese and onion in a greased 9x13-inch baking dish. Sprinkle with the chips. Mix the tomatoes and soups in a bowl. Pour over the layers. Bake at 350 degrees for 30 minutes. Yield: 8 servings.

Diann Mitchell, Doyline

Onion and Cheese Chicken

1 teaspoon seasoned salt
1 teaspoon pepper
1/4 cup melted butter
6 boneless skinless chicken breasts, about 2 pounds
1 (4-ounce) jar sliced mushrooms, drained
1 (3-ounce) can French-fried onions
1/2 cup shredded Monterey Jack, Swiss or
mozzarella cheese

Combine the seasoned salt and pepper with the butter in a small bowl. Rinse the chicken and pat dry. Roll chicken in the seasoned butter. Place in a microwave-safe dish. Cover with waxed paper. Microwave on High for 5 to 6 minutes. Turn the chicken over and top with the mushrooms. Microwave on High for 4 minutes. Top with the onions and cheese. Microwave, uncovered, on High for 2 to 3 minutes or until cooked through. Yield: 6 servings.

Genevieve Carlisle, Shreveport

Chicken and Rice Casserole

6 boneless skinless chicken breasts
1 tablespoon vegetable oil
1 cup water
1 (10-ounce) can cream of chicken soup
1 (10-ounce) can cream of mushroom soup
1 envelope onion-mushroom soup mix
1 cup uncooked rice
Salt and pepper to taste

Rinse the chicken and pat dry. Brown in the oil in a skillet; drain. Cut into small strips. Combine the water, soups, soup mix, rice and seasonings in a bowl. Pour into a 9x13-inch baking dish. Arrange the chicken on top. Bake, covered tightly with foil, at 350 degrees for 1 hour. May substitute 6 pork chops for chicken breasts. May use low-salt soups. Yield: 6 servings.

Gert Hawkins, Ventress

Chicken Spaghetti

1 (3-pound) chicken
1 medium onion, chopped
1 green bell pepper, chopped
3 ribs celery, chopped
1 cup melted butter
3 (10-ounce) cans cream of mushroom soup
16 ounces Velveeta cheese with jalapeños, cubed
1 (16-ounce) package spaghetti

Rinse the chicken. Cook the chicken in water in a stockpot until tender. Remove the chicken and reserve the broth. Remove the chicken from the bones and chop. Sauté the onion, green pepper and celery in the butter in a large skillet until tender. Add the soup and cheese. Simmer until the cheese melts, stirring often. Add the chicken. Cook the spaghetti in the reserved broth; drain. Add to the chicken mixture. Spoon into two 11x13-inch baking dishes. Bake at 350 degrees for 30 minutes. May freeze before baking. Yield: 12 servings.

Dolores Ancelet, Rayne

Chicken in Tomato Gravy

1 (3-pound) chicken, cut up
Salt and cayenne pepper to taste
1 tablespoon vegetable oil
1 large onion, chopped
1/2 cup chopped green bell pepper
1/2 cup chopped green onion tops
2 cloves of garlic, minced
1 (8-ounce) can tomato sauce
1 cup cooked lima beans

Rinse the chicken and pat dry. Season with salt and cayenne pepper. Brown in the oil in a heavy saucepan. Add the onion, green pepper, green onion tops and garlic. Sauté the vegetables until tender; drain. Add the tomato sauce and 1/2 to 1 cup water. Simmer for 30 minutes. Add the lima beans. Simmer for 15 minutes longer. Remove to a serving bowl. Adjust the seasonings in the gravy. Yield: 6 servings.

Geneviève Lyons, Church Point

Easy Chicken Stew

1 (3-pound) chicken, cut up
2 (10-ounce) cans cream of chicken soup
1/2 cup water
1 envelope onion soup mix
1 tablespoon browning sauce

Rinse the chicken and pat dry. Arrange in a greased baking dish. Combine the soup, water, soup mix and browning sauce in a bowl and mix well. Pour over the chicken. Bake at 350 degrees for 1 1/2 hours. Yield: 6 servings.

Ruth Brown, Jennings

Chicken Casserole with White Beans and Rice

1 (4-ounce) package white beans and rice mix
1 (10-ounce) can cream of chicken soup
1 soup can water
1 (5-ounce) can sliced water chestnuts, drained
1 envelope onion soup mix
6 boneless chicken breasts

Combine the white beans and rice mix, soup, water, water chestnuts and onion soup mix in a bowl. Pour into a greased 9x13-inch baking dish. Rinse the chicken and pat dry. Arrange over the rice mixture. Bake, covered with foil, at 325 degrees for 45 minutes. Check the casserole and add a small amount of water if necessary. Bake for 45 minutes longer or until beans and rice are tender and chicken is cooked through. Yield: 6 servings.

Yvonne Eastman, Jennings

Chicken and Dumplings

1 (3-pound) chicken
1 (10-ounce) can cream of chicken soup
Salt and pepper to taste
1/4 cup margarine
1 (10-count) package flour tortillas

Rinse the chicken well. Cook the chicken in water to cover in a heavy saucepan until tender. Remove the chicken, reserving the broth. Remove the chicken from the bones and set aside. Add the soup and enough water to fill the saucepan 2/3 full. Season with salt and pepper. Add the margarine. Bring the broth to a boil. Cut the tortillas into quarters. Drop into the boiling broth, separating with a fork. Cook for 5 minutes, using the fork to separate. Reduce heat and simmer for 5 to 8 minutes, continuing to use fork to separate dumplings. Stir in the chicken. Simmer until thickened to the desired consistency. Yield: 6 servings.

Courtney Bolding, Oak Grove

Bayou Bounty

Fish & Seafood

Shrimp boats bob along the docks in Venice, Louisiana. One of the last inhabitable points along Louisiana's southern most "toe," the town is reminiscent of its Italian namesake. Water surrounds the area, making it an ideal launching point for the state's shrimping fleet.

Photograph by Judy Jacobs, Baton Rouge, LA

Fish & Seafood

Baked Fish and Rice, 97
International Stuffed Catfish, 98
Light Catfish Fillets, 99
Fish Court Bouillon, 100
Snappy Garfish, 101
Poached Shark, 102
Jann's Alligator Sauce Picante, 103
RR's Alligator Sauce Picante, 104
Maw Maw's Crab Meat au Gratin, 105
Crawfish Casserole, 106
Crawfish Étouffée, 107
Easy Crawfish Étouffée, 108
Mom's Crawfish Étouffée, 109
Crawfish Fettuccini Casserole, 110
Baked Crawfish Fettucini, 110
Crawfish Pies, 111
Crawfish Quiche, 112
Low-Fat Barbecued Shrimp, 113
Shrimp Scampi, 114
Shrimp and Crab Stew, 115
Shrimp Étouffée, 116
Shrimp Fettuccini, 117
Easy Shrimp Fettuccini, 118
Quick Shrimp and Pasta, 119
Great Seafood Casserole, 120

Baked Fish and Rice

1 small onion, chopped
1/2 cup melted margarine
1 (14-ounce) can chicken broth
1 cup uncooked rice
Salt and seasoned salt to taste
1/2 teaspoon pepper
Tony Chachere's Creole seasoning to taste
4 (8-ounce) fish fillets

Sauté the onion in the margarine in a skillet until tender. Combine the onion, broth, rice and seasonings in a bowl. Spoon into a 9x13-inch baking dish. Arrange the fillets on top and press into the rice. Bake, covered, at 350 degrees for 45 minutes. Bake, uncovered, for 10 minutes longer. Yield: 4 servings.

Patricia Kincaid, Extension

International Stuffed Catfish

6 catfish fillets
Salt and black pepper to taste
1/4 teaspoon red pepper
1 tablespoon lemon juice
1/4 cup finely chopped onion
1/4 cup finely chopped green bell pepper
2 tablespoons butter
1/2 cup cream of mushroom soup
1/2 cup Mexican cheese spread
1 cup cooked rice
1/2 cup chopped crawfish tails
1 cup chopped catfish
1/4 cup finely chopped green onion tops
1/4 teaspoon thyme
1/2 teaspoon garlic powder
2 tablespoons melted butter
1 cup Italian bread crumbs

Season the fillets with salt, black pepper and red pepper. Place in a dish. Sprinkle with the lemon juice and let stand in the refrigerator. Sauté the onion and green pepper in 2 tablespoons butter in a large skillet until tender. Combine the soup and cheese and add to the skillet; mix well. Add the rice, crawfish, chopped catfish, green onions, thyme and garlic powder. Cook over low heat for 1 or 2 minutes; remove from heat. Brush each fillet with melted butter. Spread 2 teaspoons rice mixture onto each fillet. Roll up the fillets and secure with wooden picks. Roll the fillets in the remaining butter and then in bread crumbs to coat and place in a greased baking dish. Top with any remaining butter and bread crumbs. Bake at 375 degrees for 20 to 25 minutes or until fish flakes easily. May season the fish with additional herbs and seasonings of choice. Yield: 6 servings.

Regan Landry, Lake Charles

Light Catfish Fillets

1/2 cup light butter
4 catfish fillets
1 cup chopped onion
1 teaspoon paprika

Melt the butter in a small skillet. Spread on a baking sheet. Arrange the fillets in the butter, top with the onion and sprinkle with the paprika. Place the baking sheet on a gas grill. Grill the fillets for 5 minutes after the pan is hot. Turn the fillets and grill for 5 minutes longer. Yield: 4 servings.

Bonnie Pace, Natchitoches

Fish Court Bouillon

2 bunches green onions, chopped
2 large onions, chopped
1 bunch parsley, chopped
1/2 cup shortening
1/2 cup flour
4 pounds catfish fillets, cut into serving pieces
1 (6-ounce) can tomato paste
3 tablespoons chopped garlic
Tony Chachere's Creole seasoning to taste
5 cups water

Combine the green onions, onions and parsley in a small bowl. Melt 1/4 cup of the shortening in a stockpot. Layer half the flour, onion mixture, fillets and tomato paste over the shortening. Add the remaining shortening and repeat the layers. Add the garlic and seasoning. Pour the water over the layers. Simmer, covered, over low heat for 1 hour. Serve over rice. Yield: 8 servings.

Loretta Treme, Elton

Snappy Garfish

2 pounds boneless garfish
Tony Chachere's Creole seasoning to taste
1 cup cornmeal
Vegetable oil for frying
1 onion, chopped
1 green bell pepper, chopped
1 (10-ounce) can tomatoes with green chiles

Slice the fish into 2-inch pieces. Roll in a mixture of the seasoning and cornmeal. Fry in the oil in a 12-inch skillet until brown on both sides; drain, reserving 2 tablespoons oil. Sauté the onion and green pepper in the reserved oil until tender. Add the tomatoes and top with the fish. Cook, covered, over low heat for 30 to 45 minutes or until cooked through, adding water as needed to make a gravy. Serve over rice. Yield: 4 servings.

Margaret Desselle, Moreauville

Poached Shark

4 (8-ounce) shark steaks
1/2 lemon, sliced
2 cups water
2 (10-ounce) cans cream of mushroom soup
1 tablespoon chopped green onions
1 pound boiled shrimp
Salt and red pepper to taste

Poach the shark in a skillet with the lemon slices and water for 5 minutes or until tender. Stir in the soup, green onions, shrimp and seasonings. Cook for 5 minutes longer. Place in a greased 9x12-inch foil pan. Bake at 350 degrees for 15 minutes. Yield: 4 servings.

Adeline Lafleur, Bunkie

Jann's Alligator Sauce Picante

2 onions, chopped
3 ribs celery, chopped
1/4 cup vegetable oil
1/3 cup white wine Worcestershire sauce
1 (6-ounce) can tomato paste
1 cup water
1 (14-ounce) can Cajun stewed tomatoes
2 (14-ounce) cans Cajun tomato sauce
1 tablespoon minced garlic
2 tablespoons Tony Chachere's Creole seasoning
1 teaspoon salt
3 bay leaves
4 pounds alligator, cut into bite-size pieces
1/2 cup chopped green onion tops
1/3 cup chopped parsley

Sauté the onions and celery in the oil in a heavy 5-quart saucepan over low heat until tender. Add the Worcestershire sauce. Simmer for 10 minutes. Add the tomato paste and half of the water. Cook for 5 minutes, stirring constantly. Stir in the remaining water, stewed tomatoes, tomato sauce, garlic, Creole seasoning, salt and bay leaves. Simmer for 1 1/2 to 2 hours, adding water as needed. Add the alligator, green onion tops and parsley. Cook, covered, for 20 minutes or until the alligator is tender. Remove the bay leaves before serving over rice. May add green bell pepper with onions and celery if desired. Yield: 8 servings.

Jann Jones, Grand Chenier

RR's Alligator Sauce Picante

1 cup vegetable oil
2 cups flour
2 pounds onions, chopped
4 ribs celery, chopped
1 (10-ounce) can tomatoes with green chiles
1 (14-ounce) can stewed tomatoes
1 (10-ounce) can herbed tomato sauce
3 pounds alligator
Salt and pepper to taste
3 tablespoons Worcestershire sauce
2 tablespoons minced garlic
2 green bell peppers, chopped
2 ounces hot sauce
2 (10-ounce) cans golden mushroom soup
2 (8-ounce) cans mushrooms
1 pound shallots, chopped
1/2 bunch parsley

Heat the oil in a heavy 20-quart stockpot. Add the flour. Cook over low heat until light brown, stirring constantly. Add the onions. Cook for 10 minutes. Add the celery, tomatoes with green chiles, stewed tomatoes and herbed tomato sauce. Cook for 30 minutes. Cut the alligator into small pieces and sprinkle with salt and pepper to taste. Add the alligator, Worcestershire sauce, garlic, green peppers and hot sauce to the stockpot. Cook for 1 hour, adding small amounts of water as needed. Stir in the soup and mushrooms. Cook until the alligator is tender. Add the shallots, parsley, salt and pepper. Cook until heated through. May substitute pork, fish, turtle, venison or rabbit for the alligator.
Yield: 10 servings.

Stephen Hymel, Paulina

Maw Maw's Crab Meat au Gratin

2 ribs celery, chopped
1 medium onion, chopped
1/2 cup melted butter
3 tablespoons flour
1 (12-ounce) can evaporated milk
2 egg yolks, beaten
1 teaspoon salt
1/2 teaspoon red pepper
1/4 teaspoon black pepper
2 pounds crab meat
8 ounces Cheddar cheese, shredded

Sauté the celery and onion in the butter in a medium skillet until tender. Stir in the flour. Cook for several minutes but do not brown. Stir in the evaporated milk gradually. Add the egg yolks, salt, red pepper and black pepper. Simmer for 5 minutes, stirring constantly. Stir in the crab meat. Pour into a greased 9x9-inch baking dish and top with the cheese. Bake at 375 degrees for 10 to 15 minutes or until the cheese is golden brown.
Yield: 8 servings.

Jann Jones, Grand Chenier

Crawfish Casserole

1½ cups chopped onion
2 cloves of garlic, minced
1 cup chopped celery
⅓ cup chopped green bell pepper
½ cup melted margarine
1 pound cooked crawfish tails
1 (10-ounce) can cream of mushroom soup
½ cup chopped green onions
¼ cup finely chopped parsley
3 slices moistened bread, torn into small pieces
2 cups cooked rice
1 (4-ounce) can sliced mushrooms
Salt and pepper to taste
1 cup bread crumbs

Sauté the onion, garlic, celery and green pepper in the margarine in a large skillet until tender. Stir in the crawfish, soup, green onions and parsley. Cook for 20 minutes or until the crawfish tails curl. Stir in the torn bread, rice, mushrooms, salt and pepper. Pour into a 2-quart baking dish and sprinkle with the bread crumbs. Bake at 350 degrees for 20 minutes or until brown. May prepare casserole in advance and refrigerate until needed.
Yield: 4 servings.

Anne Regan, Crowley

Crawfish Étouffée

2 large onions, chopped
3 cups chopped celery
1 cup chopped green bell pepper
5 cloves of garlic, chopped
6 green onions, chopped
1½ cups melted butter
2 pounds crawfish tails
¼ cup chopped parsley
Salt, black pepper, red pepper and paprika to taste
Tony Chachere's Creole seasoning to taste
2 tablespoons flour
4 cups water

Sauté the onions, celery, green pepper, garlic and green onions in the butter in a large heavy saucepan until tender. Add the crawfish, parsley and seasonings to taste. Cook over medium heat until the crawfish tails curl and become firm. Stir in the flour. Add the water. Cook, covered, for 20 minutes or longer, stirring occasionally. Serve over rice. May increase the amount of flour for a thicker étouffée. Yield: 6 servings.

Brenda Wells, Coushatta

Easy Crawfish Étouffée

4 large onions, chopped
5 ribs celery, chopped
1 large green bell pepper, chopped
1 1/2 cups melted butter
1 (8-ounce) can tomato sauce
1 (10-ounce) can tomatoes with green chiles
2 (10-ounce) cans golden mushroom soup
Garlic powder to taste
1 teaspoon lemon juice
Worcestershire sauce to taste
1/4 cup (or more) chopped parsley
1/4 cup (or more) chopped green onion tops
4 pounds peeled crawfish

Sauté the onions, celery and green pepper in the butter in a large skillet until tender. Stir in the tomato sauce, tomatoes with green chiles, soup, garlic powder, lemon juice and Worcestershire sauce. Cook for 10 minutes. Add the parsley, green onion tops and enough water to make of the desired consistency. Stir in the crawfish. Cook for 20 to 30 minutes or until done to taste. May thicken with cornstarch if desired. Yield: 16 servings.

Marie Simon, Youngsville

Mom's Crawfish Étouffée

1½ large onions, chopped
1 green bell pepper, chopped
2 cloves of garlic, minced
2 tablespoons vegetable oil
2 teaspoons mustard
2 tablespoons roux
½ cup water
1 (8-ounce) can tomato sauce
2 pounds crawfish tails
1 (10-ounce) can cream of mushroom soup

Sauté the onions, pepper and garlic in the oil in a heavy iron saucepan until tender. Add the mustard and roux. Cook until smooth and brown, stirring constantly. Add the water. Cook for 10 minutes. Stir in the tomato sauce. Cook for 15 minutes. Add the crawfish. Cook for 20 minutes or until the crawfish tails are firm. Stir in the soup. Simmer, covered, for 20 minutes. Yield: 6 servings.

Dianna Fontenot, Eunice

Crawfish Fettuccini Casserole

3 onions, chopped
3 ribs celery, chopped
2 green bell peppers, chopped
2 cloves of garlic, chopped
1/4 cup flour
1/4 cup dried parsley
1 1/2 cups melted margarine
3 pounds peeled crawfish
2 cups half-and-half
2 tablespoons chopped jalapeños
1 pound Velveeta cheese, shredded
Salt and pepper to taste
16 ounces fettuccini, cooked
1/4 cup grated Parmesan cheese

Sauté the onions, celery, green peppers, garlic, flour and parsley in the margarine in a large skillet for 15 minutes, stirring frequently. Add the crawfish. Cook for 15 minutes. Stir in the half-and-half, jalapeños and half of the Velveeta cheese. Season with salt and pepper. Cook for 30 minutes, stirring frequently. Fold in the fettuccini. Pour into a greased baking dish. Top with the grated Parmesan cheese and the remaining Velveeta cheese. Bake at 350 degrees for 15 to 20 minutes or until bubbly. May substitute shrimp for crawfish. May prepare casserole omitting cheese topping. Add cheeses just before baking. Yield: 10 servings.

Betty A. McDonald, Tallulah

Denise Hymel of *Gramercy* prepares her **Baked Crawfish Fettucini** as the above recipe but adds an additional green bell pepper and 2 additional cloves of garlic and substitutes 1/2 cup butter for the margarine. She also omits the chopped jalapeños and Velveeta cheese in favor of using a pound of shredded Monterey Jack cheese with jalapeños. For the topping, she adds a mixture of enough shredded American cheese and Parmesan cheese to cover the fettucini.

Crawfish Pies

1 package frozen miniature pastry shells
1 large onion, chopped
1 large green bell pepper, chopped
3 ribs celery, chopped
5 cloves of garlic, chopped
1/2 cup melted margarine
1 (10-ounce) can golden mushroom soup
2 tablespoons chopped parsley
1 pound crawfish, ground
1/2 cup tomato sauce
1/2 cup bread crumbs
Salt, black pepper and red pepper to taste

Bake the pastry shells using the package directions for several minutes or until partially done. Sauté the onion, green pepper, celery and garlic in the margarine in a large skillet until tender. Add the soup, parsley, crawfish and tomato sauce. Cook for 5 minutes. Stir in the bread crumbs and seasonings. Cook for 15 minutes. Spoon into the pastry shells. Place on a baking sheet. Bake at 450 degrees for 10 minutes. Yield: 8 servings.

Vikki Cutrer, Hester

Crawfish Quiche

1 unbaked (9-inch) pie shell
1/4 cup chopped onion
1/4 cup chopped green bell pepper
1 tablespoon melted butter
3 eggs, beaten
2 1/2 cups shredded Cheddar cheese
1 teaspoon Worcestershire sauce
3/4 cup evaporated milk
Salt and pepper to taste
1 pound crawfish tails

Bake the pie shell at 400 degrees just until light brown. Sauté the onions and green peppers in the butter in a small skillet until tender. Combine with the eggs, cheese, Worcestershire sauce, evaporated milk, salt, pepper and crawfish in a large bowl. Pour into the pie shell. Bake at 350 degrees for 35 to 45 minutes or until set. Yield: 8 servings.

Nettie Spurgeon, Zachary

Low-Fat Barbecued Shrimp

1 (8-ounce) bottle liquid nonfat butter-flavor cooking spray
2 cloves of garlic, chopped
Tony Chachere's Creole seasoning to taste
2 tablespoons Worcestershire sauce
1 teaspoon liquid crab boil
2 tablespoons white wine
2 pounds (21- to 25-count) unpeeled
large shrimp without heads

Heat the cooking spray in a 9-inch skillet. Add the garlic, Creole seasoning, Worcestershire sauce, crab boil and wine. Add the unpeeled shrimp. Cook for 3 minutes or until the shrimp turn pink, stirring constantly. Serve with French bread.
Yield: 2 servings.

Thomas Dicharry, Bunkie

Shrimp Scampi

1 pound (36-count) shrimp
3/4 cup butter
1/2 teaspoon salt
3/4 teaspoon garlic powder
1 tablespoon minced parsley
1 tablespoon lemon juice
1 tablespoon minced parsley

Peel the shrimp, rinse well and pat dry with paper towels. Melt the butter in a small saucepan. Add the salt, garlic powder, 1 tablespoon of the parsley and lemon juice; mix well. Pour the butter mixture into a 9x13-inch baking pan. Arrange the peeled shrimp in a single layer in the pan. Bake at 400 degrees for 5 minutes. Turn the shrimp over. Sprinkle with the remaining tablespoon parsley. Bake for 5 minutes longer. Do not overbake. Remove the shrimp to a serving plate. Pour the garlic butter drippings over the shrimp. Yield: 3 servings.

Jim Monroe, Baton Rouge

Shrimp and Crab Stew

1/2 cup finely chopped green onions
1/4 cup finely chopped onion
1/2 green bell pepper, finely chopped
2 tablespoons vegetable oil
2 1/2 cups water
1/4 cup dry roux mix
1/2 teaspoon salt
1 teaspoon pepper
1 teaspoon Tony Chachere's Creole seasoning
1 pound shrimp, peeled, deveined
2 (6-ounce) cans white lump crab meat

Sauté the green onions, onion and green pepper in the oil in a large skillet until tender. Add the water. Simmer until the mixture is hot. Stir in the roux mix. Simmer on low for 15 minutes or until the mixture thickens. Stir in the seasonings, shrimp and crab meat. Simmer, partially covered, over low heat for 10 minutes or until the shrimp turn pink. Serve over rice or hollowed-out fried pistollette rolls. Leftovers may be frozen. Yield: 6 servings.

Linda Bordelon, Moreauville

Shrimp Étouffée

3 tablespoons flour
1/4 cup melted margarine
2 large onions, chopped
4 green onions, chopped
1/2 tablespoon minced garlic
2 tablespoons chopped parsley
1/2 (10-ounce) can tomatoes with green chiles
2 (10-ounce) cans golden mushroom soup
20 ounces water
1 pound shrimp, peeled

Blend the flour into the margarine in a large skillet. Add the onions, green onions, garlic and parsley. Cook until the vegetables are tender. Add the tomatoes, soup and water. Cook for 20 to 30 minutes. Add the shrimp. Cook for 20 minutes. Turn off the heat. Cover the skillet and let stand for 30 minutes. Serve over rice. May substitute crawfish for shrimp. May store leftovers in the refrigerator for 2 days or freeze. Yield: 4 servings.

Alice Peterson, Oak Grove

Shrimp Fettuccini

2 onions, chopped
1 green bell pepper, chopped
2 ribs celery, chopped
2 cloves of garlic, chopped
1 cup melted butter
1/4 cup flour
3 tablespoons chopped parsley
2 pounds peeled shrimp
2 cups half-and-half
1 pound jalapeño cheese, shredded
1 (16-ounce) package egg noodles, cooked
Salt and pepper to taste
1/4 cup grated Parmesan cheese

Sauté the onions, green pepper, celery and garlic in the butter in a large skillet until tender. Stir in the flour, parsley and shrimp. Cook for 10 minutes. Add the half-and-half and jalapeño cheese. Cook until the cheese melts, stirring constantly. Fold in the noodles and season with salt and pepper. Pour into a nonstick 9x13-inch baking dish and sprinkle with the Parmesan cheese. Bake at 350 degrees for 20 minutes. May substitute crab meat for shrimp. Yield: 8 servings.

Michelle Alexander, Greenwell Springs

Easy Shrimp Fettuccini

1 onion, chopped
1/2 clove of garlic, chopped
1/4 cup melted butter
2 to 3 tablespoons flour
1 pound (or more) peeled shrimp
2 cups half-and-half
1/4 cup shredded Velveeta cheese
Salt, pepper and Tabasco sauce to taste
1/4 cup chopped parsley
1/4 cup chopped green onion tops
1 (16-ounce) package fettuccini, cooked, cooled
1/4 cup grated Parmesan cheese

Sauté the onion and garlic in the butter in a large skillet until tender. Stir in the flour. Add the shrimp. Cook, uncovered, over low heat until the shrimp turn pink. Add the half-and-half, Velveeta cheese, seasonings, parsley and green onion tops. Fold in the fettuccini. Spoon into a greased baking dish. Bake at 350 degrees for 15 minutes. Sprinkle with the Parmesan cheese.
Yield: 8 servings.

Sheri DeRouen, Jeanerette

Quick Shrimp and Pasta

1 pound shrimp, peeled, deveined
2 tablespoons white wine Worcestershire sauce
Garlic powder to taste
Salt, black pepper and red pepper to taste
2 tablespoons light margarine
1 teaspoon cornstarch
1/3 cup water
1 (4-ounce) envelope noodles with
butter and herb sauce, cooked

Combine the shrimp, Worcestershire sauce, garlic powder and seasonings in a bowl. Chill, covered, for 2 hours or longer. Cook the seasoned shrimp in a 10-inch skillet coated with cooking spray and margarine until the shrimp turn pink, turning once. Mix the cornstarch and water. Stir into the shrimp mixture. Simmer, covered, for 3 or 4 minutes or until thickened, stirring constantly. Pour over the noodles in a serving bowl, tossing to mix well.
Yield: 4 servings.

Jane S. Gravois, Vacherie

Great Seafood Casserole

8 ounces cream cheese
1/2 cup margarine
1 large onion, chopped
1 green bell pepper, chopped
2 ribs celery, chopped
2 tablespoons melted margarine
1 (10-ounce) can cream of mushroom soup
1 (6-ounce) can chopped mushrooms
1 cup cooked rice
1 pound shrimp, peeled
1 pint crab meat
Salt and pepper to taste
8 ounces shredded Cheddar cheese
2 to 3 cups cracker crumbs

Melt the cream cheese and 1/2 cup margarine in a small saucepan. Sauté the onion, green pepper and celery in 2 tablespoons margarine in a large saucepan until tender. Stir in the cream cheese mixture, soup, mushrooms and rice. Season the shrimp and crab meat with salt and pepper. Add to the saucepan and adjust seasonings; mix gently. Place in a greased 3-quart casserole. Top with the cheese and cracker crumbs. Bake at 350 degrees for 20 to 30 minutes or until bubbly. Yield: 8 servings.

H. C. Zaunbrecher, Eunice

French Market Basket

Vegetables & Side Dishes

Like no other place in Louisiana, the French Market of New Orleans offers up the freshest vegetables to be found anywhere. Many of the great chefs of New Orleans can be found perusing the day's harvest, seeking more than your garden variety vegetable for the perfect side dish.

Photograph by Margaret Martinez, Prairieville, LA

Vegetables & Side Dishes

Artichokes and Tomatoes, 123
Low-Fat Asparagus Fettuccini Alfredo, 124
Toledo Bend Baked Beans, 125
Creole-Style Green Beans, 126
Bean and Artichoke Casserole, 127
Broccoli Casserole, 128
Cabbage Casserole, 129
Baked Corn, 130
Corn Casserole, 131
Chile Corn Casserole, 132
Granny's Corn Maque Choux, 133
Eggplant and Green Pepper Italian, 134
Mirliton Casserole, 135
Mirliton Pirogues, 136
Black-Eyed Pea Casserole, 137
Poke Sallet, 138
Heavenly Hash Brown Casserole, 139
Potato Casserole, 140
Squash Casserole, 141
Spinach and Artichoke Casserole, 142
Glazed Sweet Potato Casserole, 143
Holiday Sweet Potatoes, 144
Pineapple Sweet Potato Puff, 145
Sweet Potato-Banana Casserole, 146
Restuffed Sweet Potatoes, 147
Zucchini Pie, 148
Green Rice, 149
Rice and Carrot Dressing, 150
Rice Casserole, 151
Pineapple Casserole, 152
Blueberry Jelly, 153
Sweet Pickles, 153
Bread-and-Butter Pickles, 154

Artichokes and Tomatoes

1 (14-ounce) can artichoke hearts, drained
1 (14-ounce) can stewed tomatoes
1 tablespoon grated Parmesan cheese

Cut the artichoke hearts into quarters. Cook the artichokes and tomatoes in a 1-quart saucepan over medium heat for 15 minutes. Top with the cheese. May drain the tomatoes, finely chop the tomatoes and artichokes and mix well to serve as a dip with crackers. May substitute 1/4 teaspoon salt for the cheese.
Yield: 6 servings.

Charlotte Castille, Lafayette

Low-Fat Asparagus Fettuccini Alfredo

1 (3-ounce) envelope nonfat country gravy mix
2 1/2 cups water
1 cup grated fat-free Parmesan cheese
1 (7-ounce) jar roasted red peppers, or
1/2 cup, drained and chopped
1/8 teaspoon hot pepper sauce
1 (8-ounce) package fettuccini
8 ounces fresh asparagus, cut into 1-inch slices

Blend the gravy mix with 1/2 cup of the water in a bowl. Bring the remaining 2 cups water to a boil in a saucepan. Pour the gravy mixture into the boiling water. Cook until thickened, whisking constantly. Stir in the cheese, peppers and hot sauce. Remove from the heat; keep warm. Cook the fettuccini using the package directions, adding the asparagus during the last 4 minutes of cooking time. Drain the mixture and return to the saucepan. Pour the gravy mixture over the fettuccini, stirring to coat. Garnish with fresh parsley. May substitute one 10-ounce package thawed frozen broccoli for the asparagus. Yield: 6 servings.

Jann Logan, Gilliam

Toledo Bend Baked Beans

1 (52-ounce) can pork and beans
1 (2-ounce) jar honey
1 (2-ounce) bottle steak sauce
10 to 12 slices slab bacon
4 ribs celery, chopped
1 large bunch green onions, chopped
1 medium onion, chopped
1/2 cup chopped green bell pepper
8 cloves of garlic, chopped
Black pepper, red pepper and salt to taste
Tony Chachere's Creole seasoning to taste
Greek seasoning to taste
Tabasco sauce to taste

Place the pork and beans in a large baking dish. Stir in the honey and steak sauce. Fry the bacon in a large skillet until half cooked. Remove the bacon, reserving the drippings. Chop the bacon and add to the beans. Sauté the celery, green onions, onion, green pepper and garlic in the reserved pan drippings. Season generously with the black pepper, red pepper, salt, Creole seasoning, Greek seasoning and Tabasco sauce and mix well. Add the sautéed vegetables to the beans in the prepared dish and mix well. Bake at 350 degrees for 2 1/2 hours, stirring frequently. May add 1 cup barbecue sauce before baking for a zestier flavor.
Yield: 6 servings.

Reynold Minsky, Lake Providence

Creole-Style Green Beans

6 slices bacon
3/4 cup chopped onion
1/2 cup chopped green bell pepper
2 tablespoons flour
2 tablespoons brown sugar
1 tablespoon Worcestershire sauce
1/8 teaspoon dry mustard
1/2 teaspoon salt
1/4 teaspoon pepper
1 (10-ounce) can tomatoes with green chiles
1 (16-ounce) can green beans, drained

Cook the bacon in a skillet until crisp-fried. Remove the bacon; crumble and set aside, reserving 3 tablespoons bacon drippings in the skillet. Sauté the onion and green pepper in the reserved bacon drippings. Stir in the flour, brown sugar, Worcestershire sauce and dry mustard. Season with the salt and pepper. Add the tomatoes and cook until thickened, stirring constantly. Stir in the green beans. Pour into a medium baking dish. Top with the crumbled bacon. Bake at 350 degrees for 15 to 20 minutes or until bubbly. Yield: 4 servings.

Carole Mitchell, Doyline

Bean and Artichoke Casserole

3 (16-ounce) cans French-style green beans
2 (16-ounce) cans artichoke hearts, drained, mashed
1 cup grated Parmesan cheese
1 cup seasoned bread crumbs
1/3 cup olive oil

Drain the beans, reserving the juice of 1 can. Layer the beans, artichokes, cheese and bread crumbs 1/2 at a time in a 9x13-inch baking dish. Pour the reserved bean juice over the top and sprinkle with the olive oil. Bake at 375 degrees for 40 to 45 minutes or until heated through. Yield: 12 servings.

Melba McIntosh, Pioneer

Broccoli Casserole

3 (10-ounce) packages frozen broccoli
1 teaspoon onion powder
Pepper to taste
1 roll garlic cheese
1/2 cup margarine
1 (10-ounce) can cream of mushroom soup
1 cup cornflakes, crushed

Cook the broccoli in water in a saucepan until tender; drain. Chop into pieces and place in a 2-quart greased casserole. Sprinkle with the onion powder and pepper. Place the garlic cheese and margarine in a microwave-safe dish. Microwave on Medium until melted. Stir in the soup. Pour over the broccoli. Sprinkle with the cornflake crumbs. Bake at 400 degrees for 15 minutes.
Yield: 8 servings.

Marie Ory, Convent

Cabbage Casserole

1 medium head cabbage, finely chopped
1 large onion, chopped
6 tablespoons margarine
1 (10-ounce) can cream of mushroom soup
2 cups shredded Velveeta cheese
Salt and pepper to taste
1½ cups bread crumbs

Cook the cabbage in water to cover in a large saucepan until tender; drain. Sauté the onion in the margarine in a large skillet. Add the soup and cheese. Season with salt and pepper. Cook over low heat until the cheese melts, stirring constantly. Add the cabbage and mix well. Stir in 1 cup of the bread crumbs. Spoon the mixture into a 2-quart baking dish. Top with the remaining ½ cup bread crumbs. Bake at 350 degrees for 25 minutes or until bubbly. Yield: 10 servings.

Colette Gravois, Napoleonville

Baked Corn

1 egg, beaten
2/3 cup milk
1 (17-ounce) can cream-style corn
1 (16-ounce) can whole kernel corn, drained
1/2 cup chopped onion
1/2 cup chopped green bell pepper
2 pimentos, chopped
1 cup shredded sharp Cheddar cheese
1 cup cracker crumbs
1/4 cup melted butter or margarine
2 tablespoons sugar

Beat the egg with the milk in a bowl. Add the cream-style corn, whole kernel corn, onion, green pepper, pimentos, cheese, cracker crumbs, butter and sugar; mix well. Place in a 7x11-inch baking dish. Bake at 350 degrees for 1 hour. Yield: 12 servings.

Edda Hoffpauir, Lake Charles

Corn Casserole

1/4 cup margarine
2 (17-ounce) cans cream-style corn
1/2 cup finely chopped onion
1 tablespoon sugar
2 eggs, beaten
1 teaspoon salt
1 teaspoon pepper
1/2 cup water
1 (6-ounce) package Mexican corn bread mix

Melt the margarine in a 9x13-inch baking dish. Combine the corn, onion, sugar, eggs, salt, pepper, water and corn bread mix in a bowl; mix well. Spoon into the prepared baking dish. Bake at 325 degrees for 1 hour. May serve as a main dish by adding 1 pound browned ground beef before baking. Yield: 10 servings.

Carole Mitchell, Doyline

Chile Corn Casserole

16 ounces cream cheese
1/2 cup margarine
1/4 cup flour
1 cup milk
3 (16-ounce) cans whole kernel corn, drained
3 jalapeños, chopped

Melt the cream cheese and margarine in a double boiler over hot water. Stir in the flour and milk until smooth. Stir in the corn and peppers. Pour into a greased 9x13-inch baking dish. Bake at 350 degrees for 30 minutes or until bubbly. Yield: 8 servings.

Claire Carlisle, Shreveport

Granny's Corn Maque Choux

1/4 cup butter
1/2 cup bacon drippings
2 (10-ounce) packages frozen whole kernel corn
2 (17-ounce) cans cream-style corn
1 1/2 tablespoons sugar
1 cup chopped tomatoes, or
1 (10-ounce) can tomatoes with green chiles
1 cup chopped onion
1 cup chopped green bell pepper

Melt the butter with the bacon drippings in a large skillet. Add the frozen corn, 1 can of the cream-style corn, sugar, tomatoes, onion and green pepper. Cook until the mixture is slightly brown on the bottom, stirring occasionally. Add the remaining can of cream-style corn. Cook, covered, for 10 minutes longer. May substitute fresh corn for the frozen corn. Yield: 12 servings.

Loretta Treme, Elton

Eggplant and Green Pepper Italian

2 (17-ounce) cans peeled whole tomatoes
6 cloves of garlic, pressed
1 tablespoon sugar
1 tablespoon olive oil
1 tablespoon chopped fresh basil
3 tablespoons grated Romano cheese
1/2 to 1 tablespoon salt
Pepper to taste
Olive oil for frying
2 large green bell peppers, cut into small strips
1 large eggplant, thinly sliced
1 cup grated Romano cheese

Prepare the sauce by mashing the tomatoes with a fork or potato masher, reserving all the pulp and juice. Place the tomato pulp and juice in a small saucepan. Add the garlic, sugar, 1 tablespoon olive oil, basil, 3 tablespoons Romano cheese, salt and pepper. Simmer for 30 minutes. Heat 1/4 inch olive oil in a large skillet. Fry the green peppers in desired amount of olive oil until tender; remove the pepper strips from the skillet with a slotted spoon and drain. Fry the eggplant in the remaining olive oil until tender; remove and drain. Alternate layers of eggplant and green peppers in a greased 2-quart baking dish, spreading the sauce and a sprinkling of cheese between each layer and topping with sauce and cheese. Bake at 300 degrees until the cheese melts.
Yield: 6 servings.

Reynold Minsky, Lake Providence

Mirliton Casserole

7 large mirlitons, peeled, seeded
1/2 cup chopped onion
1/4 cup chopped green bell pepper
2 ribs celery, chopped
1 tablespoon canola oil
1 pound lean ground beef
Cajun seasoning to taste
1/2 cup bread crumbs

Cook the mirlitons in water to cover in a saucepan until tender; drain. Mash and set aside. Sauté the onion, green pepper and celery in the oil in a large skillet. Add the ground beef and Cajun seasoning. Cook for 10 minutes or until the ground beef is brown, stirring until crumbly. Add the mashed mirlitons and cook until most of the liquid evaporates. Place in a greased 1 1/2-quart casserole. Top with the bread crumbs and bake at 350 degrees for 35 minutes. Yield: 8 servings.

Geneviève Lyons, Church Point

Mirliton Pirogues

8 large mirlitons
1 medium onion, chopped
1/2 cup margarine
1 pound crab meat
1 cup bread crumbs
Salt and pepper to taste
1/4 cup butter

Cook the mirlitons in water to cover in a saucepan until tender; drain. Slice each mirliton lengthwise and discard the seeds. Scrape out the pulp, reserving the pulp and shells. Sauté the onion in the margarine in a skillet. Stir in the crab meat and reserved mirliton pulp. Add the bread crumbs to thicken. Season with salt and pepper. Stuff into the reserved mirliton shells. Top each with 1/2 tablespoon butter. Bake at 350 degrees for 25 minutes or until golden brown. May top with additional bread crumbs if desired. Yield: 8 servings.

Lynette P. Gravois, Hester

Black-Eyed Pea Casserole

1½ pounds ground beef
1 (16-ounce) can black-eyed peas
1 (17-ounce) can cream-style corn
1 cup buttermilk
½ cup flour
1 cup cornmeal
2 eggs, beaten
½ teaspoon baking soda
½ teaspoon salt
½ cup vegetable oil
1 medium onion, chopped
1 (4-ounce) can jalapeños, chopped
2 cups shredded Cheddar cheese

Brown the ground beef in a skillet, stirring until crumbly; drain. Combine with the peas, corn, buttermilk, flour, cornmeal, eggs, baking soda, salt, oil, onion and peppers in a bowl and mix well. Stir in 1½ cups of the cheese. Spoon into a 9x13-inch baking dish. Top with the remaining ½ cup cheese. Bake at 350 degrees for 45 minutes. Yield: 8 servings.

Kris Liles, Doyline

Poke Salad

1 pound (about) tender young poke leaves
1 chopped onion
1/4 cup margarine
Salt and pepper to taste
2 eggs, slightly beaten

Remove the stems from the poke leaves; wash the leaves thoroughly. Bring to a boil in water in a saucepan and boil for 3 minutes. Drain and repeat the process 3 or 4 times until the water is no longer green. Sauté the onion in the margarine in a skillet. Add the poke leaves and enough water to cover the bottom of the skillet. Season with salt and pepper. Cook until the poke is tender. Stir in the beaten eggs. Cook for 5 minutes, stirring constantly. Serve with corn bread. May top with sliced onion rings and sliced or chopped hard-cooked eggs. Yield: 6 servings.

Mrs. Stuart Williams, Pleasant Hill

Heavenly Hash Brown Casserole

1 large onion, chopped
1/2 cup margarine
1 (16-ounce) package frozen hash brown potatoes
Salt and red pepper to taste
1 cup sour cream
1/2 cup milk
3 cups shredded Cheddar cheese
1 (10-ounce) can cream of mushroom soup
1/2 cup melted butter
2 cups crushed cornflakes

Sauté the onion in 1/2 cup margarine in a small skillet. Combine with the potatoes in a bowl. Season with salt and red pepper. Stir in the sour cream, milk, cheese and soup. Spoon into a 9x13-inch baking dish. Mix the melted butter and cornflakes in a small bowl. Sprinkle over the top. Bake, uncovered, at 300 degrees for 45 to 60 minutes or until bubbly and brown. Yield: 10 servings.

Karen Wild, Welsh

Potato Casserole

6 large potatoes, peeled
6 tablespoons butter
8 ounces cream cheese
1 (12-ounce) can evaporated milk
1/4 cup chopped green onions
2 tablespoons bacon bits
1/2 cup shredded Cheddar cheese

Cook the potatoes in water in a saucepan until tender and drain. Add the butter and beat until smooth. Mix in the cream cheese and evaporated milk. Add the green onions and bacon bits. Place in a greased 7x11-inch baking dish. Top with the Cheddar cheese. Bake at 350 degrees for 15 to 20 minutes or until the cheese is melted and browned. Yield: 8 servings.

Betty Smith, Bossier City

Squash Casserole

5 or 6 medium yellow squash, sliced
1/2 cup chopped onion
1/2 cup margarine
1 (10-ounce) can cream of celery soup
32 butter crackers, crushed
1/2 cup grated Parmesan cheese

Sauté the squash and onion in the margarine in a large skillet until tender. Stir in the soup and cracker crumbs. Pour into a greased 2-quart baking dish. Bake at 350 degrees for 25 minutes or until bubbly. Top with the cheese and bake for 5 minutes longer. Yield: 6 servings.

Phyllis G. Moore, Jonesboro

Spinach and Artichoke Casserole

2 (10-ounce) packages frozen chopped spinach
1 onion, chopped
1/2 cup margarine
16 ounces cream cheese
2 (16-ounce) cans artichoke hearts, cut into quarters
1/2 teaspoon garlic salt
1 tablespoon Tony Chachere's Creole seasoning
1/2 cup grated Parmesan cheese
1/2 cup Italian bread crumbs

Cook the spinach using the package directions and drain well. Sauté the onion in the margarine in a large skillet until tender. Stir in the cream cheese until melted. Add the spinach, artichokes, seasonings and Parmesan cheese; mix well. Pour into a 9x13-inch baking dish. Top with the bread crumbs. Bake at 350 degrees for 30 minutes. May also serve as a dip with corn chips.
Yield: 10 servings.

Grace S. Graugnard, St. James

Glazed Sweet Potato Casserole

6 unpeeled medium sweet potatoes
1/4 cup packed brown sugar
1/4 cup honey
1 tablespoon cornstarch
1/2 teaspoon ground cinnamon
1/4 teaspoon ground nutmeg
2 teaspoons grated orange peel
2 tablespoons butter
1/2 cup pineapple juice
1/4 cup chopped walnuts

Cook the sweet potatoes in water to cover in a large saucepan for 20 to 25 minutes or until tender; let cool. Peel and cut into 1/2-inch slices. Arrange in a greased 8x12-inch baking dish. Combine the brown sugar, honey, cornstarch, cinnamon, nutmeg, orange peel, butter and pineapple juice in a small saucepan. Cook over medium heat until the mixture is thickened and bubbly, stirring constantly. Pour over the sweet potatoes and sprinkle with the walnuts. Chill, covered, for 8 hours. Let stand at room temperature for 30 minutes. Bake, uncovered, at 350 degrees for 30 minutes or until heated through. Yield: 8 servings.

Kay Haley, Oak Grove

Holiday Sweet Potatoes

3 cups mashed cooked sweet potatoes, or
2 (16-ounce) cans, drained, mashed
1 cup sugar
1/2 teaspoon salt
2 eggs, beaten
1/4 cup melted margarine
1/4 cup milk
1/4 teaspoon vanilla extract
1/4 teaspoon almond extract
1 cup packed brown sugar
1/3 cup flour
1 cup pecans, chopped
3 tablespoons melted margarine

Combine the sweet potatoes, sugar, salt, eggs, 1/4 cup margarine, milk and flavorings in a large bowl and mix well. Pour into a 9x9-inch baking dish. Combine the brown sugar, flour, pecans and 3 tablespoons margarine in a small bowl; mix well. Sprinkle over the top. Bake at 350 degrees for 30 minutes. Yield: 8 servings.

Vivian Anderson, Ethel

Pineapple Sweet Potato Puff

4 large sweet potatoes, cooked, peeled
1/4 cup low-fat margarine
2 eggs, beaten
1 cup evaporated milk
1/3 cup sugar
1/4 teaspoon salt
1 teaspoon vanilla extract
2 (20-ounce) cans sliced pineapple, drained
1/4 cup chopped pecans

Mash the sweet potatoes in a large bowl. Add the margarine, eggs, evaporated milk, sugar, salt and vanilla; mix well. Place the pineapple slices in a 9x9-inch baking dish sprayed with nonstick cooking spray. Pour in the sweet potato mixture. Top with the pecans. Bake at 350 degrees for 20 minutes. Yield: 8 servings.

Beryl Eisworth, St. Francisville

Sweet Potato-Banana Casserole

3 cups mashed cooked sweet potatoes
1/4 cup melted butter or margarine
1/2 cup packed brown sugar
1/4 cup orange juice
1/4 cup chopped pecans
1/4 cup grated coconut
2 cups mashed bananas
1/2 cup crushed cornflakes
1/4 cup packed brown sugar
2 tablespoons butter, cut into pieces

Combine the sweet potatoes, melted butter, 1/2 cup brown sugar, orange juice, pecans and coconut in a bowl and mix well. Place 1/2 of the mixture in a buttered 9x13-inch baking dish. Add the bananas and the remaining sweet potato mixture. Top with a mixture of the cornflakes and 1/4 cup brown sugar. Dot with 2 tablespoons butter. Bake at 275 degrees for 25 minutes.
Yield: 8 servings.

Geneviève Lyons, Church Point

Restuffed Sweet Potatoes

4 large sweet potatoes
1/2 cup packed brown sugar
1/2 cup melted butter
1/4 cup honey

Bake the sweet potatoes at 350 degrees for 1 hour or until tender; cool slightly. Cut a lengthwise slice from each sweet potato and scoop the pulp into a bowl, leaving the shells intact. Add the brown sugar, butter and honey to the sweet potato pulp; mix well. Spoon the mixture into the reserved shells and place in an 8x8-inch baking dish. Bake at 350 degrees for 10 to 15 minutes or until heated through. Yield: 4 servings.

Bonnie Pace, Natchitoches

Zucchini Pie

1/2 cup chopped onion
3 cups chopped zucchini
1 cup baking mix
1 egg
1/3 cup milk
1/3 cup vegetable oil
1 cup cubed Cheddar cheese
1/4 to 1/2 teaspoon seasoned salt

Sauté the onion in a nonstick skillet until tender. Combine with the zucchini, baking mix, egg, milk, oil, cheese and seasoned salt in a large bowl; mix well. Place in a 10-inch pie plate. Bake at 350 degrees for 40 minutes. Yield: 6 servings.

Katherine Moore, Jonesboro

Green Rice

2 cups uncooked rice
2/3 cup chopped green onions
1/4 cup vegetable oil
1 1/2 tablespoons Worcestershire sauce
1/4 teaspoon red pepper
2 to 4 cups beef broth

Combine the rice, green onions, oil, Worcestershire sauce, red pepper and broth in a large saucepan. Bring the mixture to a boil and cover. Simmer for 20 minutes or until tender. May cook in a rice cooker according to manufacturer's directions, using 2 cups broth. Yield: 12 servings.

Mindy Hetzel, Jennings

Rice and Carrot Dressing

1 pound carrots, scraped, sliced
1 large onion, chopped
1 cup chopped green bell pepper
2 ribs celery, chopped
3 tablespoons margarine
1/2 cup water
Salt and red pepper to taste
2 cups cooked rice

Cook the carrots in water to cover in a 2-quart saucepan until tender; drain. Sauté the carrots with the onion, green pepper and celery in the margarine in the saucepan until tender. Add the water. Simmer, covered, over medium heat for 30 minutes. Add the salt, pepper and rice and mix well. Cook until heated through. Yield: 6 servings.

Theresa T. Cormier, Breaux Bridge

Rice Casserole

1 pound ground beef
$1^1/_4$ cups uncooked rice
1 (10-ounce) can cream of mushroom soup
1 (16-ounce) can whole kernel corn, drained
1 small onion, chopped
Salt and pepper to taste
6 slices bacon

Combine the ground beef, rice, soup, corn, onion, salt and pepper in a bowl and mix well. Spoon into a greased $2^1/_2$-quart baking dish. Place the bacon across the top. Bake, covered, at 350 degrees for $1^1/_4$ hours. Bake, uncovered, for 15 minutes longer. May substitute green beans or green peas for the corn in this recipe. Yield: 6 servings.

Regina Landry, Crowley

Pineapple Casserole

2 (20-ounce) cans pineapple tidbits
1 cup shredded sharp Cheddar cheese
1 cup crushed butter crackers
1/4 cup melted butter
1/2 cup packed brown sugar
1/2 cup sugar
7 tablespoons flour

Drain the pineapple, reserving 1 cup juice. Place the pineapple in a greased 2 1/2-quart baking dish. Top with a mixture of the cheese, cracker crumbs and butter. Combine the reserved pineapple juice, brown sugar, sugar and flour in a small saucepan. Cook until the sugars dissolve and the mixture thickens, stirring constantly. Pour over the casserole. Bake at 350 degrees for 20 minutes. Serve as a side dish with ham. Yield: 8 servings.

Jody Pollard, Rayville

Blueberry Jelly

3 1/2 cups blueberry juice
1 package Sure-Jel
5 cups sugar
1 tablespoon lemon juice

Bring the blueberry juice to a boil in a saucepan. Add the Sure-Jel. Bring the juice to a hard boil. Add the sugar and lemon juice, stirring to dissolve the sugar. Boil for 1 minute or until the mixture sheets from the spoon, stirring constantly. Remove from the heat and skim off the foam. Pour into hot sterilized jelly jars, leaving 1/4-inch headspace. Seal with paraffin. May also seal with 2-piece lids and process in a boiling water bath for 10 minutes. Yield: 4 pints.

Robert Alexander, Homer

Sweet Pickles

1 (32-ounce) jar sliced dill pickles
2 cups sugar

Drain the pickles, reserving the juice. Store the reserved juice in the refrigerator. Remove the pickles from the jar. Return the pickles to the jar, sprinkling each 1/2-inch layer with sugar until all the ingredients are used. Chill, covered, for 3 days or until the sugar dissolves. Pour some of the reserved juice back into the jar. Store in the refrigerator. Yield: 32 servings.

Felton Vickers, Monroe

Bread-and-Butter Pickles

1 gallon cucumbers, sliced
8 small onions, sliced
2 green bell peppers, sliced
1/2 cup salt
4 cups sugar
1 1/2 teaspoons turmeric
1/2 teaspoon cloves
2 tablespoons mustard seeds
1 tablespoon celery seeds
5 cups vinegar

Combine the cucumbers, onions and green peppers in a large crock and sprinkle with the salt. Cover with ice and let stand for 3 hours; drain well. Mix the sugar, turmeric and cloves in a large stockpot. Add the mustard seeds, celery seeds and vinegar. Add the cucumber mixture. Heat until scalding but not boiling. Pack the cucumbers into hot sterilized jars and add the liquid, leaving 1/2-inch headspace. Seal with 2-piece lids. Process in a boiling water bath for 10 minutes. Yield: 8 pints.

Nettie Spurgeon, Zachary

Breads

This black iron stove is still used in the home of Jim Norris, of Winnsboro, Louisiana. Weekend mornings are filled with the aroma of wood and biscuits with cane syrup. Like the recipes to follow, good cooking in northeast Louisiana is most folks' bread and butter.

Photograph by Felton Vickers, Monroe, LA

Breads

Banana Bread, 157
Broccoli Corn Bread, 157
Mexican Corn Bread, 158
Poppy Seed Bread, 159
Sweet Potato Biscuits, 160
Sweet Potato Muffins, 160
Harvest Bread, 161
Sausage Bread, 162
Cheese Bread, 163
Dinner Rolls, 164

Banana Bread

1 cup sugar
1/2 cup vegetable oil
2 eggs
3 large bananas, mashed
1 cup flour
1 teaspoon baking soda
1/2 teaspoon baking powder
1/2 teaspoon salt
2 tablespoons milk
1/2 teaspoon vanilla extract

Beat the sugar, oil and eggs in a mixer bowl until smooth. Add the bananas, flour, baking soda, baking powder and salt and mix well. Add the milk and vanilla and mix well. Pour the batter into 2 loaf pans. Bake at 350 degrees for 45 minutes or until the loaves test done. Yield: 24 servings.

Mindy Hetzel, Jennings

Broccoli Corn Bread

1 (12-ounce) can whole kernel corn, drained
4 eggs, beaten
1 cup mixture of chopped onion, green bell pepper and celery
12 ounces small curd cottage cheese
1 (8-ounce) jar processed cheese spread
1/2 cup melted margarine
1 (10-ounce) package frozen chopped broccoli, thawed
1 (7-ounce) package corn bread mix
1 teaspoon Tony Chachere's seasoning

Mix the corn, eggs, onion mixture, cottage cheese, cheese spread, margarine and broccoli in a bowl. Add the corn bread mix and seasoning and mix well. Pour into a greased 9x13-inch baking pan. Bake at 400 degrees for 30 minutes. Yield: 15 servings.

Phyllis Rabalais, Morrow

Mexican Corn Bread

2 cups yellow cornmeal
1/4 cup flour
2 teaspoons baking powder
1 teaspoon baking soda
2 tablespoons sugar
1 1/2 cups buttermilk
3 slices bacon, crisp-fried and crumbled
2 tablespoons bacon drippings
1/2 cup chopped onion
4 jalapeños, seeded, chopped
1 (16-ounce) can cream-style corn
16 ounces Cheddar cheese, or process cheese, shredded

Combine the cornmeal, flour, baking powder, baking soda, sugar, buttermilk, bacon, drippings, onion, jalapeños, corn and cheese in a large bowl and mix well. Pour into a greased 9x13-inch baking pan. Bake at 450 degrees for 40 to 45 minutes or until golden brown. Yield: 15 servings.

Linda Zaunbrecher, Gueydan

Poppy Seed Bread

2 eggs
1/2 cup sugar
3/4 cup vegetable oil
1 teaspoon vanilla extract
1/4 cup poppy seeds
2 cups flour
1 teaspoon baking powder
1 teaspoon salt
1 cup evaporated milk
1 cup chopped pecans

Beat the eggs, sugar and oil in a mixer bowl until smooth. Add the vanilla and poppy seeds and mix well. Sift the flour, baking powder and salt into a medium bowl. Add to the egg mixture alternately with the evaporated milk, mixing well after each addition. Stir in the pecans. Pour into 2 greased and floured 4x8-inch loaf pans. Bake at 325 degrees for 1 1/4 hours. Remove from the oven and let stand for 5 minutes. Remove the loaves from the pans and cool on a wire rack. Yield: 24 servings.

Melba McIntosh, Pioneer

Sweet Potato Biscuits

2 1/2 cups baking mix
1/3 cup margarine
1/2 cup milk
1 cup mashed cooked sweet potatoes

Combine the baking mix, margarine and milk in a bowl. Add the sweet potatoes and mix well. Drop the dough by heaping tablespoonfuls onto a floured surface and shape into biscuits. Place on a baking sheet. Bake at 275 degrees for 15 minutes or until golden brown. Store the leftover biscuits in sealable plastic bags in the refrigerator. Yield: 6 servings.

Pam Bouillion, Rayne

Sweet Potato Muffins

1 cup mashed cooked sweet potatoes
2 tablespoons margarine or butter, softened
1 cup baking mix
1 teaspoon cinnamon
1 teaspoon nutmeg
1/4 cup honey
2 eggs
1/3 cup sugar
1 cup chopped pecans

Combine the sweet potatoes, margarine, baking mix, cinnamon, nutmeg, honey, eggs, sugar and pecans in a bowl and mix well. Pour into muffin cups sprayed with nonstick cooking spray or lined with paper muffin cups. Bake at 350 degrees for 35 minutes. May glaze with a mixture of confectioners' sugar and milk.
Yield: 12 servings.

Penny Bouquet, Baker

Harvest Bread

2 envelopes dry yeast
1 cup soy flour
1 cup whole wheat flour
1/2 cup all-purpose flour
1/4 cup wheat germ
3 cups warm (105- to 115-degree) water
3/4 cup nonfat dry milk
3 1/2 cups (or more) all-purpose flour
2 tablespoons sugar
1 tablespoon brown sugar
1 tablespoon salt
2 tablespoons shortening, dissolved in hot water

Combine the yeast, soy flour, whole wheat flour, 1/2 cup all-purpose flour and wheat germ in a mixer bowl. Add the warm water and nonfat dry milk. Beat at medium speed for 2 minutes, scraping the side of the bowl occasionally. Mix in 3 1/2 cups flour, sugar, brown sugar, salt and shortening, changing from mixer to hand mixing when dough becomes stiff and adding additional flour to make the dough pliable if necessary. Knead on a floured cloth for 8 to 10 minutes. Place in a greased bowl, turning to coat surface. Let rise, covered, until doubled in bulk. Punch the dough down and let rest, covered, for 15 minutes. Shape into 2 loaves and place on a baking sheet. Let rise for 30 to 40 minutes or until doubled in bulk. Bake at 375 degrees for 1 hour or until loaves test done. Cool on a wire rack. *Note:* May shape the dough into rolls after it has rested, let rise for 30 to 40 minutes and bake at 400 degrees for 12 to 15 minutes or until golden brown. Yield: 40 servings.

Patsy Granger, Jennings

Sausage Bread

1 pound hot sausage, crumbled
1 pound mild sausage, crumbled
1 pound hickory-smoked sausage, chopped
3 bunches green onions, chopped
1 (4-ounce) can mushrooms
4 cups shredded Cheddar cheese
4 cups shredded mozzarella cheese
2 cups grated Parmesan cheese
1 (4-ounce) can chopped black olives
1 (7-ounce) jar pitted green olives, chopped
Chopped jalapeños (optional)
1 (3-loaf) package frozen bread dough, thawed
1/4 cup melted butter

Brown the sausages together in a large saucepan, stirring frequently and adding the green onions and mushrooms before the sausage is cooked through. Drain and set aside. Combine the Cheddar, mozzarella and Parmesan cheeses in a large bowl. Add the olives, jalapeños and sausage mixture to the cheese mixture; mix well and set aside. Flatten one loaf of the bread dough to the size of a dinner plate on a floured surface. Place 1/3 of the sausage and cheese mixture in the middle of the bread. Bring up the sides to enclose the filling; pinch the seams to seal. Follow the same procedure for the remaining 2 loaves. Place 2 of the loaves seam side down in a lightly greased 9x13-inch baking pan and place the remaining loaf in a smaller pan. Brush with melted butter. Bake at 350 degrees for 30 minutes or until golden brown.
Yield: 36 servings.

Variations:
For an appetizer or party food, spread the sausage and cheese mixture in crescent rolls.

For a pizza loaf, spread pizza sauce on the bread before adding the sausage and cheese mixture.

Brenda Wells, Coushatta

Cheese Bread

1/2 cup light mayonnaise
1/2 cup chopped black olives
2 cloves garlic, pressed or chopped
1/2 cup light margarine, softened
6 green onions, chopped
2 cups shredded Monterey Jack cheese
1 1/2 cups sliced fresh mushrooms
1 loaf French bread

Combine the mayonnaise, olives, garlic, margarine, chopped green onions, cheese and mushrooms in a bowl and mix well. Slice the bread into halves lengthwise and place with cut sides up on a baking sheet. Spread with the cheese mixture. Bake at 350 degrees for 15 minutes. May prepare and store in the refrigerator until time to heat. May also slice the bread diagonally before baking, allowing the cheese to melt down the sides and eliminating the need to slice while hot. Yield: 10 servings.

Marilyn Wade, Farmerville

Dinner Rolls

3 to 4 cups bread flour
1 envelope dry yeast
1/4 cup sugar
1 teaspoon salt
2 tablespoons vegetable oil
1 cup milk, scalded
1/4 cup melted butter

Place 2 cups of the flour in a large bowl. Add the yeast, sugar and salt and mix well. Add the oil and scalded milk and mix well. Add enough of the remaining flour to form a thick dough. Knead on a floured surface until stiff. Place the dough in a greased bowl, turning to coat surface. Let rise, covered, for 1 to 1 1/2 hours or until doubled in bulk. Shape into rolls and place on a greased baking sheet. Let rise for 30 to 45 minutes or until doubled in bulk. Bake at 350 degrees for 20 to 25 minutes or until golden brown. Brush the tops of rolls with melted butter. Yield: 36 servings.

Priscilla Gragg, Bell City

Sweet Dreams

Cakes & Pies

The Louisiana State Capitol building stands behind moss-draped oaks and magnolias. The Capitol building, begun in 1930 by Huey P. Long and completed in 1932, is the tallest capitol in the United States. It provides panoramic views of the city and the Mississippi River from it's 27th floor observation deck.

Photograph by Sheila McCant, Baton Rouge, LA

Cakes & Pies

Sugarless Applesauce Cake, 167
Banana Cake, 168
Banana Pineapple Cake, 169
Blueberry Cake, 170
Buttermilk Cake, 170
Coconut Dream Cake, 171
Fresh Cranapple Cake, 171
Fig Cake, 172
Italian Cream Cake, 173
Lemon Poppy Seed Cake, 174
Mandarin Orange Cake, 175
Old-Fashioned Cajun Syrup Cake, 175
Fresh Peach Cake, 176
Pear Cake, 177
Pineapple Cake, 177
Cream Cheese Pound Cake, 178
Pound Cake, 178
Pumpkin Roll, 179
Red Velvet Cake, 180
Sad Cake, 181
Sweet Potato Cake, 182
So-Good Cake, 183
Frosting for German Chocolate Cake, 183
Sugar-Free Apple Pie, 184
French Coconut Pie, 185
Milk Chocolate Candy Bar Pie, 185
Cool Fruit Pies, 186
Candied Pecan Pie, 186
Best-Ever Pecan Pie, 187
Pecan Fudge Pie, 188
Rich Pecan Pie, 189
Nuttier Pecan Pie, 190

Sugarless Applesauce Cake

1 cup raisins
1 cup mixed dried fruit
2 cups water
2 cups flour
1 teaspoon baking soda
1 teaspoon cinnamon
1/2 teaspoon nutmeg
1/2 teaspoon salt
4 packets artificial sweetener
1 teaspoon vanilla extract
2 eggs
1 cup unsweetened applesauce
3/4 cup vegetable oil

Combine the raisins and dried fruit with the water in a saucepan. Cook, uncovered, until all the liquid is absorbed by the fruit. Set the fruit aside and let cool to lukewarm. Combine the flour, baking soda, cinnamon, nutmeg, salt, artificial sweetener, vanilla, eggs, applesauce and oil in a large bowl and mix well. Add the fruit and mix well. Pour into a greased 10-inch tube or bundt pan. Bake at 350 degrees for 35 to 40 minutes or until the cake tests done. Yield: 16 servings.

Dolores Ancelet, Rayne

Banana Cake

1/2 cup shortening
1 1/2 cups sugar
1 or 2 eggs
1 cup mashed banana
1 teaspoon vanilla extract
2 cups flour
1 teaspoon baking soda
1 teaspoon baking powder
1/2 teaspoon salt
3/4 cup milk

Cream the shortening and sugar in a mixer bowl until light and fluffy. Beat in the eggs, banana and vanilla. Mix the flour, baking soda, baking powder and salt together. Add to the banana mixture alternately with the milk, mixing well after each addition. Pour into a greased and floured 10x15-inch cake pan. Bake at 350 degrees for 45 minutes. Yield: 18 servings.

H. C. Zaunbrecher, Eunice

Banana Pineapple Cake

3 cups flour
2 cups sugar
1 teaspoon baking soda
1 teaspoon salt
1 teaspoon cinnamon
3 eggs
1 1/4 cups vegetable oil
1 (8-ounce) can crushed pineapple
1 cup chopped pecans
2 cups mashed bananas
1 teaspoon vanilla extract

Combine the flour, sugar, baking soda, salt and cinnamon in a large bowl. Make a well in the center of the dry ingredients and add the eggs, oil, undrained pineapple, pecans, bananas and vanilla; stir until well mixed. Pour into a greased and floured tube pan. Bake at 350 degrees for 1 1/4 hours. Yield: 16 servings.

Jennie Lee Moore, Oak Grove

Blueberry Cake

1 cup butter, softened
2 cups sugar
1 teaspoon vanilla extract
4 eggs
3 cups flour
1/2 teaspoon salt
1 teaspoon baking powder
1 pint fresh blueberries, or 12 ounces frozen, thawed

Cream the butter, sugar and vanilla in a mixer bowl until light and fluffy. Beat in the eggs 1 at a time. Combine 2 cups of the flour with the salt and baking powder. Add to the egg mixture and beat well. Toss the blueberries with the remaining 1 cup flour. Fold gently into the batter. Spoon into a greased, floured and sugared tube pan. Bake at 325 degrees for 1 1/4 hours. Yield: 16 servings.

Linda Drain, Plaquemine

Buttermilk Cake

1 cup shortening
3 cups sugar
1 teaspoon (or more) vanilla extract
5 eggs   1 cup buttermilk
1/2 teaspoon baking soda
3 cups sifted flour

Cream the shortening, sugar and vanilla at high speed in a mixer bowl until light and fluffy. Add the eggs one at a time, beating well after each addition. Combine the buttermilk and baking soda in a bowl. Add to the egg mixture alternately with the flour. Pour into a greased and floured 10-inch bundt or tube pan. Bake at 325 degrees for 1 hour and 20 minutes; do not open the oven door during the first hour of baking. Cool in the pan on a wire rack for 20 minutes. Loosen the edges and remove to the wire rack to cool completely. Yield: 16 servings.

Judy G. Jacobs, Baton Rouge

Coconut Dream Cake

1 (2-layer) package white or yellow cake mix
1 (16-ounce) can cream of coconut
12 ounces whipped topping
1 (7-ounce) can flaked coconut

Prepare and bake the cake mix using the package directions for a 9x13-inch cake pan. Cool for 20 minutes. Poke holes in the cake with the handle of a wooden spoon. Pour the cream of coconut over the cake. Top with whipped topping and coconut. Chill until serving time. Yield: 15 servings.

Candy Carlisle, Shreveport

Fresh Cranapple Cake

1 cup canola oil
2 1/4 cups sugar
3 eggs, beaten
2 teaspoons vanilla extract
3 cups flour
1 teaspoon baking soda
1/2 teaspoon salt
1 teaspoon cinnamon
2 cups chopped apples
2 cups fresh whole cranberries
2 cups coarsely chopped pecans

Beat the oil and sugar in a large mixer bowl. Beat in the eggs and vanilla. Add the flour, baking soda, salt and cinnamon, mixing well. Stir in the apples, cranberries and pecans by hand. Pour into a greased and floured bundt pan. Bake at 325 degrees for 1 1/4 hours. Yield: 12 servings.

Marilyn Wade, Farmerville

Fig Cake

2 cups sugar
1 cup vegetable oil
3 eggs
1 teaspoon vanilla extract
1 cup mashed fig preserves
2 cups flour
1 teaspoon baking soda
1/2 teaspoon cinnamon
1/2 teaspoon allspice
1/8 teaspoon salt
2/3 cup buttermilk
2 cups finely chopped pecans

Beat the sugar and oil in a mixer bowl. Beat in the eggs one at a time. Add the vanilla and fig preserves, beating well. Sift the flour, baking soda, cinnamon, allspice and salt in a medium bowl. Add to the fig mixture alternately with the buttermilk, mixing well after each addition. Stir in the pecans by hand. Pour into a greased and floured tube pan. Bake at 325 degrees for 1 1/2 hours. Yield: 16 servings.

Margaret Martinez, Prairieville

Italian Cream Cake

5 egg whites
1/2 cup margarine, softened
1/2 cup shortening
2 cups sugar
5 egg yolks
1 teaspoon baking soda
1 cup buttermilk
2 cups flour
1 (7-ounce) can coconut
1 teaspoon vanilla extract
1 cup chopped pecans
Cream Cheese Frosting

Beat the egg whites in a mixer bowl until stiff and set aside. Cream 1/2 cup margarine, shortening and sugar in a mixer bowl until light and fluffy. Beat in the egg yolks one at a time. Combine the baking soda and buttermilk in a small bowl. Add to the creamed mixture alternately with the flour, mixing well after each addition. Stir in the coconut, 1 teaspoon vanilla and pecans. Fold in the egg whites. Pour into 3 greased and floured 9-inch cake pans. Bake at 325 for 35 minutes. Cool on wire racks. Spread Cream Cheese Frosting between the layers, and over the top and side of cake. Yield: 12 servings.

Cream Cheese Frosting

1/2 cup margarine, softened
8 ounces cream cheese, softened
1 teaspoon vanilla extract
1 pound confectioners' sugar

Cream 1/2 cup margarine and cream cheese in a mixer bowl until light and fluffy. Beat in 1 teaspoon vanilla and confectioners' sugar until smooth.

Mindy Hetzel, Jennings

Lemon Poppy Seed Cake

1 (2-layer) package 97% fat-free yellow cake mix
1/2 cup sugar
1/3 cup vegetable oil
1/4 cup water
1 cup nonfat plain yogurt
1 cup egg substitute
3 tablespoons lemon juice
2 tablespoons poppy seeds
Lemon Glaze

Combine the cake mix and sugar in a large mixer bowl. Add the oil, water, yogurt, egg substitute and 3 tablespoons lemon juice. Beat at medium speed for 6 minutes. Stir in the poppy seeds by hand. Pour into a bundt pan coated with cooking spray. Bake at 350 degrees for 40 minutes or until the cake tests done. Cool in the pan on a wire rack for 10 minutes. Remove from the pan and cool completely. Drizzle the Lemon Glaze over the top of the cake. Yield: 24 servings.

Lemon Glaze

1/2 cup sifted confectioners' sugar
2 tablespoons lemon juice

Combine the confectioners' sugar and 2 tablespoons lemon juice in a small bowl, stirring until smooth.

Pam Broussard, New Iberia

Mandarin Orange Cake

3 (8-ounce) cans mandarin oranges
1 (2-layer) package yellow cake mix
16 ounces frozen whipped topping
1 (6-ounce) package vanilla instant pudding
1 (20-ounce) can crushed pineapple, drained

Drain the oranges, reserving the juice. Prepare the cake mix using the package directions, substituting the reserved mandarin orange juice for the water. Stir in 2 cans of the drained mandarin oranges. Pour into 3 greased and floured 9-inch cake pans. Bake at 300 to 325 degrees until the layers test done. Cool on wire racks. Beat the whipped topping and pudding mix in a mixer bowl until light and fluffy. Fold in the pineapple and remaining 1 can of drained mandarin oranges. Spread between the layers and over the top and side of the cake. Yield: 16 servings.

Penny Bouquet, Baker

Old-Fashioned Cajun Syrup Cake

1 cup raisins   2 1/2 cups flour
1/2 cup shortening   1 1/2 cups molasses
2 eggs   1 teaspoon cinnamon
1 teaspoon allspice
2 teaspoons ginger   1/4 teaspoon salt
1 cup boiling water
1 1/4 teaspoons baking soda

Toss the raisins in the flour and set aside. Beat the shortening, molasses and eggs in a mixer bowl until smooth. Add the cinnamon, allspice, ginger and salt. Combine the boiling water and baking soda in a bowl. Add to the molasses mixture and beat well. Stir in the raisins. Pour into a greased and floured 9-inch cake pan. Bake at 350 degrees for 35 to 40 minutes or until the cake tests done. Cool in the pan for several minutes. Remove to a wire rack and cool completely. Yield: 6 servings.

Betty Petticrew, Iowa

Fresh Peach Cake

1 cup butter or margarine, softened
2 cups sugar
3 eggs
3 cups flour
2 teaspoons baking soda
2 teaspoons cinnamon
2 cups puréed peaches
3/4 cup peach juice
2 teaspoons butter flavoring
Creamy Butter Filling and Topping

Cream 1 cup butter and 2 cups sugar in a mixer bowl until light and fluffy. Add the 3 eggs one at a time, beating well after each addition. Add 3 cups flour, baking soda and cinnamon, beating well. Stir in the peaches, juice and 2 teaspoons flavoring, mixing well. Pour into 3 greased and floured 9-inch cake pans. Bake at 350 degrees for 25 minutes. Remove to wire racks to cool. Spread the Creamy Butter Filling and Topping between the layers and over the top and side of the cake. Yield: 16 servings.

Creamy Butter Filling and Topping

2 tablespoons flour
1 cup sugar
1 cup cream
1/2 cup butter, softened
1 egg, beaten
1 teaspoon vanilla extract
1 teaspoon butter flavoring

Mix 2 tablespoons flour and 1 cup sugar in a bowl. Stir in the cream gradually. Add the 1/2 cup butter, 1 egg and flavorings, beating until smooth. Cook in a double boiler over hot water until thickened, stirring constantly. Cool slightly.

Sue Benoit, Rayne

Pear Cake

1/2 cup shortening
1/2 cup sugar
1 1/2 cups warm stewed pears
1 cup raisins 2 cups sifted flour
2 teaspoons baking soda
1 teaspoon cinnamon
1 teaspoon nutmeg or allspice
1/2 teaspoon ground cloves
1/2 teaspoon salt 1 1/2 cups pecans

Cream the shortening and sugar in a mixer bowl until light and fluffy. Add the pears and raisins, mixing well. Cool to room temperature. Sift the flour, baking soda, cinnamon, nutmeg, cloves and salt in a medium bowl. Add to the pear mixture gradually, mixing well. Stir in the pecans. Pour into a greased loaf pan. Bake at 325 degrees for 1 hour. Remove from the loaf pan and cool on a wire rack. Yield: 12 servings.

Mrs. Glen Robinson, Jonesboro

Pineapple Cake

1 (2-layer) package white cake mix
1 (6-ounce) package vanilla instant pudding mix
1 1/2 cups milk
8 ounces cream cheese
1 (20-ounce) can crushed pineapple, drained
8 ounces whipped topping
1/2 cup chopped pecans

Prepare and bake the cake mix using the package directions for a 9x13-inch cake. Cool in the pan on a wire rack. Beat the pudding mix, milk and cream cheese in a mixer bowl until smooth. Spread over the top of the cooled cake. Spread the pineapple evenly over the cream cheese. Top with the whipped topping. Sprinkle with pecans. Chill until serving time. Yield: 15 servings.

Marie Simon, Youngsville

Cream Cheese Pound Cake

8 ounces cream cheese
1 1/2 cups butter, softened
3 cups sugar
6 eggs
2 teaspoons vanilla extract
3 cups flour

Beat the cream cheese, butter and sugar in a mixer bowl until light and fluffy. Beat in the eggs 2 at a time. Add the vanilla and mix well. Add the flour gradually, mixing well. Pour into a greased and floured bundt pan. Place in a cold oven. Bake at 325 degrees for 1 1/2 to 2 hours or until the cake tests done. Remove to a wire rack to cool. Yield: 16 servings.

Wanda Benton, Tickfaw

Pound Cake

2 cups butter, softened
3 1/2 cups sugar
10 eggs
4 cups flour

Cream the butter in a mixer bowl until light. Add the sugar gradually, beating constantly until fluffy. Add the eggs 1 at a time, beating well after each addition. Stir in the flour, mixing well. Pour into a greased and floured tube pan. Bake at 300 to 325 degrees for 1 hour or until the cake tests done. Remove to a wire rack to cool. Yield: 16 servings.

Robert Alexander, Homer

Pumpkin Roll

2/3 cup mashed cooked pumpkin
3 eggs
1 cup sugar
1 teaspoon cinnamon
1 teaspoon pumpkin pie spice
1/2 teaspoon nutmeg
1/2 teaspoon ground cloves
3/4 cup self-rising flour
1/4 cup chopped pecans
2 to 4 tablespoons confectioners' sugar
Cream Cheese Filling

Combine the pumpkin, eggs, sugar, cinnamon, pie spice, nutmeg, cloves and flour in a large bowl and mix well. Pour into a greased 10x15-inch cake pan lined with greased waxed paper. Sprinkle with the pecans. Bake at 375 degrees for 15 minutes. Invert onto a damp towel sprinkled with a small amount of confectioners' sugar. Roll the cake as for a jelly roll in the towel and cool completely. Unroll the cooled cake. Spread the Cream Cheese Filling on the cake and reroll. Wrap in foil and chill until serving time. Yield: 12 servings.

Cream Cheese Filling

8 ounces cream cheese, softened
1 cup confectioners' sugar
1 teaspoon vanilla extract
2 tablespoons melted margarine

Mix the cream cheese, confectioners' sugar, vanilla and margarine in a medium mixer bowl until smooth.

Elsie Schexnayder, St. James

Red Velvet Cake

½ cup shortening
1½ cups sugar
2 eggs, at room temperature   2 cups flour
1 tablespoon baking cocoa
½ teaspoon salt   1 cup buttermilk
1 teaspoon vanilla extract
2 ounces red food coloring
1 teaspoon baking soda   1 tablespoon vinegar
Red Velvet Frosting
1 cup flaked coconut

Cream the shortening and sugar in a mixer bowl until light and fluffy. Add the eggs one at a time, beating well after each addition. Sift the flour, cocoa and salt into a medium bowl 3 times. Add to the creamed mixture alternately with the buttermilk, mixing well after each addition. Add 1 teaspoon vanilla and food coloring, mixing well. Dissolve the baking soda in the vinegar. Stir into the batter. Pour into 2 greased and floured 9-inch cake pans. Bake at 350 degrees for 30 to 35 minutes or until the layers test done. Remove to a wire rack to cool. Spread the Red Velvet Frosting between the layers and over the top and side of the cake. Sprinkle with the coconut. Yield: 16 servings.

Red Velvet Frosting

1 cup milk   ¼ cup flour
Salt to taste
½ cup shortening
½ cup margarine, softened
2 cups confectioners' sugar
1 teaspoon vanilla extract

Combine the milk, flour and salt in a saucepan. Cook over low heat until thickened, stirring constantly. Remove from the heat and cool. Cream the shortening, margarine and confectioners' sugar in a mixer bowl until light and fluffy. Beat in 1 teaspoon vanilla. Add to the cooked mixture and beat until smooth.

Joanne Bolding, Oak Grove

Sad Cake

1 (16-ounce) package light brown sugar
1/2 cup margarine
2 eggs
2 cups baking mix
1 teaspoon vanilla extract
3 tablespoons dark corn syrup
1 to 2 cups pecans
1 cup flaked coconut
1 cup chocolate chips

Combine the brown sugar and margarine in a saucepan. Cook over low heat until the margarine is melted and the brown sugar is dissolved, stirring constantly. Remove from the heat and cool. Add the eggs, baking mix, vanilla and corn syrup, mixing well. Stir in the pecans, coconut and chocolate chips. Pour into a greased and floured cake pan. Bake at 350 degrees for 45 minutes. Cool on a wire rack. Cut into squares. May vary by using the pecans, coconut and chocolate chips in any combination or proportions. Yield: 15 servings.

Michelle Soileau, Ville Platte

Sweet Potato Cake

1½ cups vegetable oil
2 cups sugar
4 egg yolks, lightly beaten
¼ cup hot water
2½ cups sifted cake flour
1 tablespoon baking powder
¼ teaspoon salt
1½ cups grated uncooked sweet potato
1 teaspoon vanilla extract
1 (8-ounce) can crushed pineapple
4 egg whites
Coconut Cream Cheese Frosting

Beat the oil and sugar in a mixer bowl until smooth. Add the egg yolks and hot water, beating well. Combine the flour, baking powder and salt. Add to the egg mixture and mix well. Stir in the sweet potato, 1 teaspoon vanilla and pineapple. Beat the egg whites in a small mixer bowl until stiff. Fold into the batter until thoroughly combined. Pour into 3 greased and floured 8-inch cake pans. Bake at 350 degrees for 25 minutes or until the cake tests done. Remove to a wire rack to cool. Spread Coconut Cream Cheese Frosting between the layers and over the top and side of the cake. Yield: 16 servings.

Coconut Cream Cheese Frosting

8 ounces cream cheese, softened
½ cup margarine, softened
1 (1-pound) package confectioners' sugar
2 teaspoons vanilla extract
1 cup flaked coconut
½ cup chopped pecans

Beat the cream cheese, margarine and confectioners' sugar in a mixer bowl until light and fluffy. Stir in 2 teaspoons vanilla, coconut and pecans.

Joanne Bolding, Oak Grove

So-Good Cake

1 (2-layer) package yellow cake mix
1 egg
1/2 cup melted butter
1 cup chopped pecans
1 (1-pound) package confectioners' sugar
8 ounces cream cheese, softened
2 eggs

Combine the cake mix, 1 egg and butter in a medium bowl, mixing well. Stir in the pecans. Press evenly over the bottom and up the sides of a greased 9x13-inch cake pan. Beat the confectioners' sugar, cream cheese and 2 eggs at medium speed in a mixer bowl until smooth. Pour into the prepared pan. Bake at 350 degrees for 30 to 35 minutes or until the top is light brown; the center will remain creamy. Cool completely. Cut into squares.
Yield: 15 servings.

Dianna Haring, Winnsboro

Frosting for German Chocolate Cake

1 1/2 cups evaporated milk
1 1/2 cups sugar
3 egg yolks, lightly beaten
1/2 cup butter, softened
1 teaspoon vanilla extract
2 1/2 cups flaked coconut
1 cup chopped pecans

Combine the evaporated milk, sugar, egg yolks, butter and vanilla in a saucepan. Cook over medium heat for 12 minutes, stirring constantly. Stir in the coconut and pecans. Remove from the heat and cool until thick enough to spead easily, stirring occasionally. Yield: 2 1/2 cups.

Stephanie Bieber-Speyrer, Church Point

Sugar-Free Apple Pie

1/3 cup thawed frozen apple juice concentrate
4 packets artificial sweetener
2 teaspoons cornstarch
1 teaspoon ground cinnamon
1 recipe (2-crust) pie pastry
8 cups thinly sliced peeled baking apples
1 tablespoon margarine

Combine the apple juice, artificial sweetener, cornstarch and cinnamon in a small bowl and set aside. Place one pastry in a 9-inch pie dish. Add the apples. Dot with the margarine. Pour the juice mixture over the apples. Top with the remaining pastry. Cut vents in the top and seal the edges. Bake at 375 degrees for 35 minutes. Increase the oven temperature to 400 degrees and bake for 15 to 20 minutes longer or until the apples are tender. Cool on a wire rack. Yield: 8 servings.

Dolores Ancelet, Rayne

French Coconut Pie

3 egg whites
1 1/2 cups sugar
1/2 cup melted butter
4 teaspoons vinegar
1 teaspoon vanilla extract
1 (3-ounce) can flaked coconut
1 unbaked (9-inch) pie shell

Beat the egg whites in a mixer bowl until stiff. Add the sugar, butter, vinegar, vanilla and coconut, beating well. Spoon into the pie shell. Bake at 350 degrees until set. Cool on a wire rack. Yield: 8 servings.

Betty Petticrew, Iowa

Milk Chocolate Candy Bar Pie

8 milk chocolate candy bars
8 ounces whipped topping
1 (9-inch) graham cracker pie shell

Place the unwrapped chocolate bars in a large microwave-safe bowl. Microwave the chocolate bars on High for 30 seconds or until crumbly; do not melt. Fold in the whipped topping. Spoon into the pie shell. Chill until serving time. May use chocolate bars that are plain or with nuts as preferred. Yield: 6 servings.

Sheila Costello, Oak Grove

Cool Fruit Pies

8 ounces cream cheese, softened
1 (14-ounce) can sweetened condensed milk
2 tablespoons lemon juice
12 ounces whipped topping
2 (16-ounce) cans sliced peaches, chopped, drained
2 (20-ounce) cans pineapple chunks, drained
1/2 cup coarsely chopped pecans
2 baked (9-inch) pie shells

Mix the cream cheese, condensed milk and lemon juice in a mixer bowl until smooth. Beat in the whipped topping. Stir in the peaches, pineapple and pecans. Spoon into the pie shells. Garnish with cherries. Chill, covered, until serving time. Yield: 16 servings.

Pam Bouillion, Rayne

Candied Pecan Pie

Favorite pecan pie filling recipe
2 cups pecans
Favorite pie shell recipe

Preheat the oven to 450 degrees. Prepare your favorite pecan pie filling recipe, substituting 2 cups of pecans for the usual amount. Pour into the pie shell. Bake for 5 minutes. Open the oven door and continue to bake for an additional 5 minutes. Reduce the oven temperature to 275 degrees. Bake in a closed oven for an additional 2 hours. Cooking at a low temperature over this amount of time candies the filling and toasts the pecans. Yield: 8 servings.

Michelle Soileau, Ville Platte

Best-Ever Pecan Pie

1/2 cup butter
1 cup light corn syrup
1 cup sugar
3 eggs, beaten
1/2 teaspoon lemon juice
1 teaspoon vanilla extract
Salt to taste
1 cup chopped pecans
1 unbaked (10-inch) pie shell

Heat the butter in a saucepan just until golden brown. Remove from heat and let cool. Combine the corn syrup, sugar, eggs, lemon juice, vanilla, salt and pecans in a bowl and mix well. Stir in the browned butter. Pour into the pie shell. Bake at 425 degrees for 10 minutes. Reduce the oven temperature to 325 degrees. Bake for 40 minutes longer. Cool on a wire rack. Yield: 8 servings.

Betty Jo Brian, Zachary

Pecan Fudge Pie

1 1/4 cups light corn syrup
1/2 cup sugar
1/3 cup baking cocoa
1/3 cup flour
1/4 teaspoon salt
3 eggs
3 tablespoons butter, softened
1 1/2 teaspoons vanilla extract
1 cup chopped pecans
1 unbaked (9-inch) pie shell

Beat the corn syrup, sugar, cocoa, flour, salt, eggs and butter in a mixer bowl until smooth. Stir in the pecans. Pour into the pie shell. Bake at 350 degrees for 45 to 50 minutes or until set. Cool on a wire rack. Garnish with whipped cream. Yield: 8 servings.

Pam Holloway, Marion

Rich Pecan Pie

1 1/2 cups sugar
1/4 cup flour
1 cup light corn syrup
2 tablespoons butter or margarine, softened
4 eggs
1 teaspoon vanilla extract
1 cup pecan halves
1 unbaked (9-inch) deep-dish pie shell

Beat the sugar, flour and corn syrup in a mixer bowl until smooth. Add the butter and eggs, beating well. Stir in the vanilla and pecans. Pour into the pie shell. Bake at 350 degrees for 1 1/4 hours. Cool on a wire rack. Yield: 8 servings.

Frances Davis, Shreveport

Nuttier Pecan Pie

3 eggs, lightly beaten
1 cup corn syrup
1 cup sugar
2 tablespoons melted margarine
1 teaspoon vanilla extract
3 cups chopped pecans
1 unbaked (9-inch) pie shell

Combine the eggs, corn syrup, sugar, margarine and vanilla in a large bowl and mix well. Stir in the pecans. Pour into the pie shell. Bake at 350 degrees for 50 to 55 minutes or until a knife inserted halfway between the center and edge comes out clean. Cool on a wire rack. Yield: 8 servings.

Sue Benoit, Rayne

Forbidden Indulgences

Candy, Cookies & Desserts

A bonfire lights up the December sky along the levee in Gramercy, Louisiana. Bonfires have been a tradition in South Louisiana for decades. Elaborate designs are constructed, such as pyramids, log homes, and reindeer, only to be burned, lighting the way for Papa Noel.

Photograph by Judy Jacobs, Baton Rouge, LA

Candy, Cookies & Desserts

Divinity, 193
Cocoa Cheese Fudge, 194
Foolproof Dark Chocolate Fudge, 194
Microwave Peanut Brittle, 195
Microwave Peanut Butter Fudge, 195
Pecan Delights, 196
Pecan Log, 196
Pralines, 197
Sweet Potato Pralines, 197
Yam Candy, 198
Toffee Crisps, 198
Brown Sugar Cookies, 199
Chinese Chews, 199
Chocolate Chip Crisp Cookies, 200
Forgotten Cookies, 200
Fannie Farmer Bars, 201
Old-Fashioned Tea Cakes, 202
Oatmeal Cookies, 203
Peanut Butter Cookies, 204
Peanut Butter Soybean Cookies, 204
Pecan Fingers, 205
Persimmon Cookies, 206
Pfefferneusse, 207
Best Sand Tarts, 208
Stir Me Nots, 208
Special Cookies, 209
Frosted Sugar Cookies, 210
Sugar Cookies, 211
Whoppers Cookies, 211
The World's Best Cookie, 212
Easy Blueberry Cobbler, 213
Banana Pudding, 213
Bread Pudding, 214
Rum Sauce for Bread Pudding, 214
Caramel Bread Pudding, 215
Caramel-Pecan Cheesecake, 216
Pineapple Cream Cheesecake, 217
Chocolate Éclair Dessert, 218
Cushaw Dessert, 218
Dutch Babies, 219
Layered Dessert, 219
Lemon Mousse, 220
Oreo Delight, 220
Peach Kuchen, 221
Pecan Pie Dessert, 222
Surprise, 222
The Best Rice Pudding, 223
Yam Parfait, 224

Divinity

2¼ cups sugar
⅓ cup light corn syrup
¼ teaspoon salt
⅓ cup water
2 egg whites
1 teaspoon vanilla extract
1 cup chopped pecans or walnuts

Combine the sugar, corn syrup, salt and water in a heavy 2-quart saucepan. Cook over medium high heat until the sugar is dissolved, stirring constantly. Cook over medium heat to 250 to 268 degrees on a candy thermometer, hard-ball stage; do not stir, wiping any sugar crystals from the side of the saucepan. Beat the egg whites in a mixer bowl until stiff. Add the hot syrup gradually, beating at medium speed until fluffy. Add the vanilla and beat until the mixture begins to lose its gloss and a small amount dropped from a spoon holds soft peaks. Fold in the pecans. Drop the candy by teaspoonfuls onto waxed paper or spoon into a lightly buttered 8-inch square pan. Let stand until set. May add a few drops of hot water if the candy becomes too stiff. Yield: 24 servings.

Betty P. Kirby, Zachary

Cocoa Cheese Fudge

2 cups margarine
1 pound Velveeta cheese, cubed
4 pounds confectioners' sugar
3/4 cup baking cocoa
1 teaspoon vanilla extract
1 1/2 cups chopped pecans

Combine the margarine and cheese in a heavy saucepan. Heat over medium heat until the mixture is melted, stirring frequently. Sift the confectioners' sugar and cocoa together into a large bowl. Add the cheese mixture, kneading until well mixed. Add the vanilla and pecans and mix well. Spread in a nonstick 10x15-inch pan or bundt pan. Chill until firm. Cut into squares. May place in 4 small gelatin molds and give as gifts. Yield: 30 servings.

Donnette W. Bennett, Spearsville

Foolproof Dark Chocolate Fudge

3 cups semisweet chocolate chips
1 (14-ounce) can sweetened condensed milk
Salt to taste
1/2 to 1 cup pecans, chopped
1 1/2 teaspoons vanilla extract

Combine the chocolate chips, condensed milk and salt in a heavy saucepan. Heat over low heat until the chocolate is melted, stirring frequently. Remove from the heat. Stir in the pecans and vanilla. Spread in a waxed-paper lined 8-inch pan. Chill for 2 hours or until firm. Invert onto a cutting board and cut into squares. Store, loosely covered, at room temperature. Yield: 24 servings.

Pam Holloway, Marion

Microwave Peanut Brittle

1 cup raw peanuts
1 cup sugar
1/2 cup light corn syrup
1/4 teaspoon salt
1 teaspoon margarine
1 1/2 teaspoons vanilla extract
1 teaspoon baking soda

Combine the peanuts, sugar, corn syrup and salt in a 1 1/2-quart microwave-safe dish. Microwave on High for 4 minutes and stir well. Microwave on High for 4 minutes longer. Stir in the margarine and vanilla. Microwave on High for 1 minute. Stir in the baking soda gently. Pour into a 10x15-inch pan sprayed with non-stick cooking spray. Let cool for 30 minutes and break into pieces. Cool completely and store in an airtight container.
Yield: 12 servings.

Pam Little, Bastrop

Microwave Peanut Butter Fudge

2 cups sugar
2 tablespoons baking cocoa
1 (5-ounce) can evaporated milk
1/2 cup margarine, cut into pieces
3/4 cup peanut butter
1/2 (10-ounce) package miniature marshmallows
1 tablespoon vanilla extract

Combine the sugar, cocoa, evaporated milk and margarine in a microwave-safe bowl. Microwave on High for 4 minutes and stir. Microwave on High for 4 minutes longer and stir. Microwave on High for 3 minutes longer. Stir in the peanut butter, marshmallows and vanilla until the marshmallows are melted. Pour into a buttered 9x13-inch dish. Let stand until firm and cut into squares.
Yield: 24 servings.

Sharlee Schexnayder, Paulina

Pecan Delights

12 large graham crackers
1 cup butter
1/2 cup sugar
1/2 cup finely chopped or ground pecans

Arrange the graham crackers in a 10x15-inch baking pan. Combine the butter and sugar in a saucepan. Bring to a boil, stirring frequently. Cook for 2 minutes, stirring frequently. Pour over the graham crackers. Sprinkle with the pecans. Bake at 350 degrees for 8 minutes. Remove from the oven and immediately cut into servings. Remove to a wire rack to cool completely. Store in an airtight container. Yield: 48 servings.

Gloria T. Moore, Elm Grove

Pecan Log

3 cups sugar
1 tablespoon butter
1 cup evaporated milk
1 cup (or more) chopped dates
2 cups pecans

Combine the sugar, butter and evaporated milk in a saucepan. Bring to a boil. Cook for 5 to 7 minutes, stirring frequently. Add the dates. Cook to 234 to 240 degrees on a candy thermometer, soft-ball stage, stirring constantly and mashing the dates. Stir in the pecans and remove from the heat. Beat until the candy cools. Spread on a dampened dish towel. Shape with the towel to form a log. Cut into slices. Yield: 12 servings.

Doris Schexnaydre, Schriever

Pralines

6 cups sugar
2 cups evaporated milk
1/2 cup butter
2 tablespoons vanilla extract
6 cups pecans

Caramelize 2 cups of the sugar in a heavy saucepan over medium heat until golden brown, stirring constantly. Combine the remaining 4 cups sugar and evaporated milk in a heavy 6-quart saucepan. Bring to a boil, stirring occasionally. Add gradually to the caramelized sugar, stirring constantly. Cook to 234 to 240 degrees on a candy thermometer, soft-ball stage. Remove from the heat. Stir in the butter, vanilla and pecans. Beat until the mixture thickens. Drop by tablespoonfuls onto waxed paper. Let stand until firm. Yield: 80 servings.

Denise Hymel, Gramercy

Sweet Potato Pralines

3 cups sugar
1 cup light cream
1 1/4 cups mashed cooked sweet potatoes
Salt to taste
1 cup packed brown sugar
2 cups broken pecans

Combine the sugar, cream, sweet potatoes and salt in a saucepan and mix well. Cook over medium heat until the mixture reaches 230 to 234 degrees on a candy thermometer, spun thread stage, stirring occasionally. Melt the brown sugar in a heavy skillet over medium heat, stirring constantly. Add to the sweet potato mixture. Stir in the pecans. Remove from the heat. Drop by tablespoonfuls onto greased pans. Yield: 20 servings.

Kay Haley, Oak Grove

Yam Candy

2 cups sugar
1/2 cup evaporated milk
1/4 cup margarine
1/2 cup mashed cooked yams
1 cup chopped pecans
1/2 teaspoon vanilla extract
3 tablespoons marshmallow creme

Combine the sugar, evaporated milk and margarine in a saucepan. Bring to a boil. Cook for 2 to 3 minutes, stirring frequently. Add the yams and pecans. Cook until the mixture starts to crystalize, stirring frequently. Remove from the heat. Add the vanilla and marshmallow creme and beat until the mixture loses its gloss. Pour into a buttered dish. Cool until firm. Cut into squares. Yield: 42 servings.

Kay Haley, Oak Grove

Toffee Crisps

12 (or more) graham crackers
1 1/2 to 2 cups chopped pecans and slivered almonds
1 cup butter or margarine
1 cup packed light brown sugar

Line a 10x15-inch nonstick baking pan with graham crackers. Sprinkle with the pecans and almonds. Combine the butter and brown sugar in a saucepan. Bring to a boil, stirring frequently. Boil for 3 minutes, stirring constantly. Pour over the nuts and graham crackers. Bake at 350 degrees for 10 minutes. Cool slightly. Cut into strips. Remove to a wire rack to cool completely. Store in an airtight container. Yield: 48 servings.

Alice Peterson, Oak Grove

Brown Sugar Cookies

1 (1-pound) package dark brown sugar
1/2 cup shortening
1/2 cup margarine, softened
2 eggs
2 cups flour
1/2 teaspoon salt
1/2 teaspoon baking soda
1 teaspoon vanilla extract
2 to 3 cups broken pecans

Cream the brown sugar, shortening and margarine in a mixer bowl until light and fluffy. Add the eggs. Beat for 1 minute. Add the flour, salt, baking soda and vanilla and mix well. Stir in the pecans. Drop by teaspoonfuls onto a greased cookie sheet. Bake at 375 degrees for 9 minutes. Cool on the cookie sheet for several minutes. Remove to a wire rack to cool completely.
Yield: 72 servings.

Margaret Desselle, Moreauville

Chinese Chews

3/4 cup flour
1 teaspoon baking powder
1/4 teaspoon salt
1 cup sugar
1 cup pecans, finely chopped
1 cup dates, finely chopped
2 eggs, beaten
3/4 teaspoon vanilla or almond extract

Combine the flour, baking powder, salt and sugar in a bowl and mix well. Stir in the pecans and dates. Add the eggs and vanilla and mix well. Spread the mixture 1/2 inch thick on a large cookie sheet with sides. Bake at 350 degrees for 30 minutes or until golden brown. Cool slightly and cut into squares. Yield: 24 servings.

Pearl Slaughter, Baker

Chocolate Chip Crisp Cookies

1¼ cups sifted flour
½ teaspoon baking soda
¼ teaspoon salt
½ cup margarine, softened
1 cup sugar
1 egg
1 teaspoon vanilla extract
2 cups crisp rice cereal
1 cup chocolate chips

Sift the flour, baking soda and salt together. Cream the margarine and sugar in a mixer bowl until light and fluffy. Add the egg and vanilla and beat well. Add the flour mixture and beat well. Stir in the cereal and chocolate chips. Drop by teaspoonfuls onto a greased cookie sheet. Bake at 350 degrees for 8 to 10 minutes or until golden brown. Remove to a wire rack to cool.
Yield: 48 servings.

Lacey Hetzel, Jennings

Forgotten Cookies

2 egg whites
1 teaspoon vanilla extract
¾ cup packed brown sugar
2 cups chopped pecans

Beat the egg whites in a mixer bowl until soft peaks form. Add the vanilla and brown sugar gradually, beating until stiff. Fold in the pecans. Drop by teaspoonfuls onto a greased and foil-lined cookie sheet. Bake at 250 degrees for 30 minutes. Turn off the oven heat. Let the cookies stand in the closed oven for 1 hour. Store in an airtight container. Yield: 48 servings.

Cindy D. Martin, Paulina

Fannie Farmer Bars

1/2 cup baking cocoa
1/2 cup butter or margarine
1/2 teaspoon salt
1 cup sugar
2/3 cup flour
2 eggs, beaten
1 teaspoon vanilla extract
1/2 (10-ounce) package miniature marshmallows
1/2 cup packed brown sugar
1/4 cup water
3 tablespoons margarine
1/4 cup baking cocoa
1 1/2 cups confectioners' sugar
1 teaspoon vanilla extract

Combine the cocoa, butter and salt in a saucepan. Heat until the butter is melted, stirring frequently. Sift the sugar and flour into a bowl. Add the eggs and 1 teaspoon vanilla and mix well. Stir into the cocoa mixture. Spoon into a greased 9x13-inch baking dish. Bake at 325 degrees until the layer tests done. Sprinkle with miniature marshmallows. Bake until the marshmallows are softened. Spread evenly over the baked layer. Combine the brown sugar, water, margarine and cocoa in a saucepan. Cook for 3 minutes, stirring frequently. Beat in the confectioners' sugar and 1 teaspoon vanilla. Drizzle over the baked layer. Cut into small squares. Yield: 36 servings.

Billie Mitchell, Doyline

Old-Fashioned Tea Cakes

2 cups margarine, softened
2 cups sugar
4 eggs, beaten
1 teaspoon baking soda
1/4 cup buttermilk
1 teaspoon vanilla extract
2 teaspoons nutmeg
6 cups flour

Cream the margarine and sugar in a large bowl. Add the eggs, baking soda, buttermilk, vanilla and nutmeg and mix well. Add the flour gradually, mixing well after each addition. Roll 1/2 inch thick on a lightly floured surface. Cut with a cookie cutter dipped in flour, using as little flour as possible. Place on a nonstick cookie sheet. Bake at 300 degrees for 10 minutes or until brown. Remove to a wire rack to cool. May freeze in a roll and thaw for 8 to 10 hours in the refrigerator before slicing and baking.
Yield: 48 servings.

Donna R. Shields, Iowa

Oatmeal Cookies

1 cup shortening
1 cup sugar
1 cup packed brown sugar
2 eggs, beaten
1 teaspoon vanilla extract
1½ cups flour
1 teaspoon salt
1 teaspoon baking soda
3 cups quick-cooking oats

Cream the shortening, sugar and brown sugar in a mixer bowl until light and fluffy. Add the eggs and vanilla and mix well. Add the flour, salt and baking soda and mix well. Add the oats 1 cup at a time, mixing well after each addition. Shape into long thin rolls. Chill, wrapped in waxed paper for up to 24 hours. Cut into slices and place on a nonstick cookie sheet. Bake at 400 degrees for 5 minutes. Remove immediately to a wire rack to cool. Store loosely covered. Yield: 72 servings.

Jewell Williams, Pleasant Hill

Peanut Butter Cookies

1 cup sugar
1 cup peanut butter
1 egg

Combine the sugar, peanut butter and egg in a bowl and mix well. Drop by teaspoonfuls onto an ungreased cookie sheet. Bake at 350 degrees for 10 minutes. Remove to a wire rack to cool. Yield: 18 servings.

Phyllis G. Moore, Jonesboro

Peanut Butter Soybean Cookies

1/2 cup shortening
1/2 cup peanut butter
1/2 cup packed brown sugar
1/2 cup sugar
1 egg
1 1/2 cups flour
1/2 teaspoon salt
1 teaspoon baking soda
1/2 teaspoon vanilla extract
1/2 cup soybeans, toasted

Cream the shortening, peanut butter, brown sugar and sugar in a mixer bowl until light and fluffy. Add the egg and mix well. Add the flour, salt, baking soda and vanilla and mix well. Stir in the soybeans. Shape into small balls and place on a greased cookie sheet. Flatten with a fork dipped in flour. Bake at 375 degrees for 10 to 12 minutes or until brown. Remove to a wire rack to cool. Yield: 60 servings.

Karen Lemoine, Hamburg

Pecan Fingers

1 cup baking mix
1/4 cup butter, softened
1 tablespoon sugar
1/4 cup chopped pecans
1/2 teaspoon vanilla extract
3 tablespoons boiling water

Combine the baking mix, butter and sugar in a bowl and mix well. Add the pecans and vanilla and mix well. Add the boiling water, stirring with a fork until mixture forms a ball. Shape into small rolls and place on an ungreased cookie sheet. Bake at 375 degrees for 10 to 12 minutes or until brown. Remove to a wire rack to cool. Yield: 24 servings.

Anne Regan, Crowley

Persimmon Cookies

½ cup butter, softened
1 cup sugar
1 teaspoon baking soda
1 cup persimmon pulp
2 cups flour
1 cup chopped pecans
1 cup raisins
1 teaspoon cinnamon
1 egg, beaten

Cream the butter and sugar together in a mixer bowl until light and fluffy. Dissolve the baking soda in the persimmon pulp in a bowl and mix until the soda is dissolved. Mix the flour, pecans and raisins in a bowl. Add to the persimmon mixture and mix well. Stir in the cinnamon and egg. Drop by teaspoonfuls onto a greased cookie sheet. Bake at 350 degrees for 12 to 15 minutes or until brown. Remove to a wire rack to cool. Yield: 24 servings.

Henrietta Landry, Elton

Pfefferneusse

1 cup margarine
1 2/3 cups honey
2 eggs, beaten
3 1/2 teaspoons baking soda
1/3 cup water
10 cups flour
2 cups sugar
2 teaspoons baking powder
1/4 teaspoon cloves
1 1/2 teaspoons cinnamon
1 teaspoon cardamon
1 teaspoon salt

Combine the margarine and honey in a saucepan. Heat over medium heat until the margarine is melted, stirring occasionally. Cool completely. Add the eggs to the cooled mixture. Stir the baking soda into the water until dissolved. Add to the honey mixture and mix well. Mix the flour with 1/2 cup of the sugar in a large bowl. Mix the remaining 1 1/2 cups sugar, baking powder, cloves, cinnamon, cardamon and salt in a medium bowl. Add to the flour mixture. Stir in the honey mixture. Chill, covered, for 8 to 10 hours. Knead the dough with lightly greased hands. Shape into 1x1 1/2-inch rolls and place on a greased cookie sheet. Bake at 350 degrees for 10 to 12 minutes or until light brown. Remove to a wire rack to cool. Yield: 120 servings.

H. C. Zaunbrecher, Eunice

Best Sand Tarts

1 cup unsalted butter, softened
1/2 cup confectioners' sugar
2 cups flour
1 tablespoon water
1 tablespoon vanilla extract
1 cup pecans, chopped

Cream the butter in a mixer bowl. Add the confectioners' sugar and flour gradually, beating until fluffy. Add the water and vanilla and mix well. Stir in the pecans. Shape into balls and place on an ungreased cookie sheet. Bake at 300 degrees for 15 to 20 minutes or until light brown. Roll in additional confectioners' sugar while hot. Place on a wire rack to cool. Yield: 36 servings.

Leslie Hanks, Lafayette

Stir Me Nots

1/2 cup melted margarine
1 1/2 cups graham cracker crumbs
1 (7-ounce) can shredded coconut
1 cup semisweet chocolate chips
1 cup butterscotch chips
1 cup chopped pecans or walnuts
1 (14-ounce) can sweetened condensed milk

Layer the margarine, graham cracker crumbs, coconut, chocolate chips, butterscotch chips and pecans in a greased 9x13-inch baking dish. Drizzle with condensed milk. Bake at 350 degrees for 35 to 40 minutes or until golden brown. Cool and cut into bars. Yield: 36 servings.

Dolores Ancelet, Rayne

Special Cookies

2 cups flour
1 teaspoon baking powder
1 teaspoon baking soda
1/4 teaspoon salt
1 cup butter, softened
2 cups packed brown sugar
2 eggs
2 cups rolled oats
2 cups coconut
2 cups chopped orange slice candy
1 cup chopped walnuts
1/2 cup semisweet chocolate chips

Sift the flour, baking powder, baking soda and salt together. Cream the butter in a mixer bowl until light. Add the sugar gradually, beating until fluffy. Beat in the eggs. Stir in the oats, coconut, orange slice candy, walnuts and chocolate chips. Add the flour mixture and mix well. Drop by teaspoonfuls onto a greased cookie sheet. Bake at 350 degrees for 15 to 20 minutes or until light brown. Remove to a wire rack to cool. Yield: 48 servings.

Linda Bordelon, Moreauville

Frosted Sugar Cookies

1 cup butter or margarine, softened
1 cup confectioners' sugar
1 egg, beaten
1½ teaspoons almond extract
1 teaspoon vanilla extract
2½ cups flour
1 teaspoon salt
3 cups confectioners' sugar
6 tablespoons butter, softened
1 teaspoon vanilla extract
2 to 4 tablespoons milk

Cream the butter and confectioners' sugar in a mixer bowl until light and fluffy. Add the egg and the almond and vanilla extracts; beat well. Combine the flour and salt in a bowl and mix well. Add to the butter mixture and beat well. Chill, covered, for 1 to 2 hours. Roll the dough to ⅛-inch thickness on a lightly floured surface. Cut with a cookie cutter dipped in flour. Place on a greased cookie sheet. Bake at 375 degrees for 7 to 9 minutes or until light brown. Remove to a wire rack to cool. Combine the confectioners' sugar and butter in a mixer bowl and mix well. Add the vanilla and enough milk to make a creamy frosting. Spread on cooled cookies. May add food coloring or sprinkle cookies with tinted sugar.
Yield: 72 servings.

Dana Bennett, Spearsville

Sugar Cookies

1 cup butter, softened
1 1/2 cups confectioners' sugar
1 egg   2 1/2 cups flour
1 teaspoon baking soda
1 teaspoon cream of tartar
1/2 cup sugar

Cream the butter and confectioners' sugar in a mixer bowl until light and fluffy. Add the egg, flour, baking soda and cream of tartar and beat well. The mixture will be stiff. Chill, covered, in the refrigerator. Shape the dough into small balls. Roll in the sugar and press between waxed paper to flatten. Place on a greased cookie sheet. Bake at 350 degrees for 12 to 15 minutes or until light brown around the edges. Remove to a wire rack to cool. Store in an airtight container. Yield: 30 servings.

Zuba Chrisman, Oak Grove

Whoppers Cookies

1 cup margarine, softened
3/4 cup packed brown sugar
3/4 cup sugar   2 eggs
2 teaspoons vanilla extract
2 1/4 cups flour
1 teaspoon baking soda
Salt to taste
2 1/4 cups crushed Whoppers candy

Cream the margarine, brown sugar and sugar in a mixer bowl until light and fluffy. Add the eggs and vanilla and beat well. Mix the flour, baking soda and salt together. Add to the sugar mixture and beat well. Stir in the candy. Drop by tablespoonfuls onto a nonstick cookie sheet. Bake at 350 degrees for 10 minutes or until light brown; do not overbake. Remove to a wire rack to cool. Yield: 36 servings.

Kathy Warren, Oak Grove

The World's Best Cookie

1 cup butter, softened
1 cup sugar
1 cup packed brown sugar
1 egg
1 cup vegetable oil
1 cup rolled oats
1 cup crushed cornflakes
1/2 cup coconut
1 cup chopped pecans
3 1/2 cups flour
1 teaspoon baking soda
1 teaspoon salt
1 teaspoon vanilla extract
1/2 cup confectioners' sugar, sifted

Cream the butter, sugar and brown sugar in a mixer bowl until light and fluffy. Add the egg and oil and beat well. Stir in the oats, cornflakes, coconut and pecans. Sift the flour, baking soda and salt together. Add to the sugar mixture. Add the vanilla and mix well. Shape into 1-inch balls and place on a nonstick cookie sheet. Flatten with a fork. Bake at 325 degrees for 12 minutes or until light brown. Remove to a wire rack to cool. Sprinkle with confectioners' sugar. Store in an airtight container.
Yield: 96 servings.

Roger V. Moseley, Ringgold

Easy Blueberry Cobbler

1/2 cup light margarine
1 cup flour
1 1/2 cups sugar
1 tablespoon baking powder
2/3 cup milk
4 cups fresh or frozen blueberries

Melt the margarine in a 9x13-inch baking dish in a 350 degree oven. Mix the flour, 1 cup of the sugar and baking powder in a bowl. Add the milk and mix well. Spread in the prepared pan. Combine the blueberries with the remaining 1/2 cup sugar in a 2-quart saucepan. Cook over medium heat until the sugar is dissolved, stirring gently. Spread over the batter. Bake at 350 degrees for 30 to 35 minutes or until brown. Yield: 10 servings.

Frances Brasher, Converse

Banana Pudding

1 (14-ounce) can sweetened condensed milk
1 1/2 cups water
1 (6-ounce) package vanilla instant pudding mix
16 ounces whipped topping
30 (or more) vanilla wafers
3 or 4 bananas, sliced

Combine the sweetened condensed milk, water and pudding mix in a bowl and mix well. Chill, covered, for 5 minutes. Stir in 1 cup of the whipped topping. Layer the vanilla wafers, bananas and pudding mixture 1/2 at a time in a serving dish. Top with remaining whipped topping. Chill until serving time.
Yield: 8 servings.

Darleen Gravois, Lutcher

Bread Pudding

9 slices bread, crumbled
1 cup raisins
1 cup sugar
1 (12-ounce) can evaporated milk
2 cups milk
4 egg yolks
1 tablespoon vanilla extract
1/3 cup melted margarine
4 egg whites
1/4 cup sugar

Mix the bread and raisins in a 9x13-inch baking dish. Combine 1 cup sugar, evaporated milk, milk, egg yolks, vanilla and margarine in a bowl and mix well. Pour over the bread and raisins. Bake at 450 degrees for 15 minutes. Beat the egg whites in a mixer bowl until soft peaks form. Add the remaining 1/4 cup sugar gradually, beating until stiff. Spread over the pudding. Bake for 3 to 4 minutes longer or until the meringue is golden brown.
Yield: 15 servings.

Elsie Schexnayder, St. James

Rum Sauce for Bread Pudding

3/4 cup margarine, softened
1 1/2 cups sugar
1 egg, beaten
1 1/2 jiggers rum

Combine the margarine and sugar in a double boiler. Cook over hot water until the sugar is dissolved, stirring constantly. Remove from the heat. Stir a small amount of the hot mixture into the beaten egg. Add the egg to the hot mixture, beating well. Cook until thickened, stirring constantly. Beat in the rum. Serve warm over bread pudding. Yield: 8 servings.

Elaine Parker, Athens

Caramel Bread Pudding

2 cups chopped apples
1 teaspoon cinnamon
1/4 teaspoon nutmeg
3 tablespoons butter
1/4 cup apple juice
1/3 cup raisins
1 teaspoon vanilla extract
1 (12-ounce) can evaporated milk
3 eggs
1/2 cup packed brown sugar
4 cups bread cubes
1/2 cup walnuts
1 teaspoon cinnamon
1/4 teaspoon nutmeg
2 tablespoons sugar

Combine the apples, 1 teaspoon cinnamon, 1/4 teaspoon nutmeg and butter in a saucepan. Cook over medium heat for 5 minutes, stirring frequently. Add the apple juice, raisins, vanilla, evaporated milk, eggs, brown sugar and bread cubes, mixing well. Pour into an 8-inch square baking dish. Process the walnuts with the remaining 1 teaspoon cinnamon, 1/4 teaspoon nutmeg and sugar in a blender. Sprinkle over the pudding. Bake at 350 degrees for 30 minutes. Yield: 8 servings.

Codie Ray, Tallulah

Caramel-Pecan Cheesecake

24 ounces cream cheese, softened
3/4 cup sugar
1 cup chopped pecans
4 eggs
1 1/2 teaspoons vanilla extract
12 ounces sour cream
1/2 cup sugar
3/4 teaspoon vanilla extract
1/2 cup chopped pecans
1 (8-ounce) jar caramel topping

Combine the cream cheese, sugar, pecans, eggs and vanilla in a mixer bowl. Beat for 5 minutes or until light and fluffy. Pour into a greased 10-inch springform pan. Bake at 350 degrees for 35 to 40 minutes or until almost firm. Remove from the oven and let stand to cool for 20 minutes. Combine the sour cream, sugar and vanilla in a bowl. Spread over the cheesecake. Bake for 15 minutes longer. Let stand to cool completely. Sprinkle the pecans over the top of the cheesecake. Drizzle with the caramel topping. Chill until serving time. Yield: 12 servings.

Margaret Brewster, Dubach

Pineapple Cream Cheesecake

1 (2-layer) package cake mix
1/2 cup melted margarine
1 egg
1 cup chopped pecans
1 (16-ounce) can crushed pineapple, drained
8 ounces cream cheese, softened
2 eggs
1 (1-pound) package confectioners' sugar

Combine the cake mix, margarine, 1 egg and pecans in a bowl. Press over the bottom of a greased 9x13-inch baking dish. Spread the pineapple evenly over the cake mixture. Beat the cream cheese, remaining 2 eggs and confectioners' sugar in a bowl. Pour over the pineapple. Bake at 350 degrees for 45 minutes or until golden brown. Let stand to cool. Yield: 15 servings.

H. C. Zaunbrecher, Eunice

Chocolate Éclair Dessert

2 (4-ounce) packages vanilla instant pudding mix
3½ cups milk
12 ounces whipped topping
16 ounces graham crackers
1 (16-ounce) can chocolate frosting

Mix the pudding with the milk in a mixer bowl. Blend in the whipped topping. Line a 9x13-inch dish with ⅓ of the graham crackers. Layer the pudding and remaining crackers ½ at a time in the prepared dish. Remove the foil top from the frosting. Microwave the frosting on High for 1 minute. Spread over the graham crackers. Chill for 24 hours or longer before serving.
Yield: 20 servings.

Erin A. Sirmon, Baton Rouge

Cushaw Dessert

1 medium cushaw, cut and peeled
1 cup margarine
3 cups sugar
½ cup flour
2 tablespoons vanilla extract
1 teaspoon lemon juice
2 eggs, beaten
1 teaspoon cloves or other spices

Boil the cushaw in water to cover in a saucepan until tender. Drain and mash. Combine the cushaw and margarine in a mixer bowl while the cushaw is still hot enough to melt the margarine. Combine the sugar and flour. Stir into the cushaw. Add the vanilla, lemon juice, eggs and cloves and mix well. Spoon into a greased 9x13-inch baking dish. Bake at 350 degrees for 20 to 30 minutes or until a wooden pick inserted comes out clean.
Yield: 10 servings.

Pearl Slaughter, Baker

Dutch Babies

3 eggs
1 cup milk
1/4 cup sugar
1 cup flour
5 tablespoons butter
1/2 cup (or more) blueberries

Process the eggs in a blender for 2 minutes. Add the milk. Blend for 2 minutes. Add the sugar and flour. Blend for 3 minutes. Melt the butter in a 10-inch cast-iron skillet in a 400-degree oven. Pour the batter into the prepared skillet. Sprinkle the blueberries over the top. Bake for 20 to 25 minutes or until browned. Serve with confectioners' sugar. Yield: 6 servings.

Tammy Rumbaugh, Benton

Layered Dessert

1 1/2 cups (or less) chopped pecans
1 1/2 cups flour
1 cup margarine, melted
8 ounces cream cheese, softened
1 cup confectioners' sugar
16 ounces whipped topping
2 (4-ounce) packages chocolate fudge instant pudding mix
3 cups milk

Combine the pecans, flour and margarine in a bowl and mix well. Press into a greased 9x13-inch baking dish. Bake at 350 degrees for 15 minutes. Cool and then chill. Beat the cream cheese and confectioners' sugar in a mixer bowl. Fold in 8 ounces of the whipped topping. Spread over the crust and chill. Prepare the pudding mix using package directions, reducing milk to 3 cups. Spread over the cream cheese. Top with the remaining whipped topping. Chill until ready to serve. Garnish with pecans.
Yield: 12 servings.

Gayle Boudreaux, Lebeau

Lemon Mousse

1 (4-ounce) package lemon instant pudding mix
1 1/2 cups cold low-fat milk
1 cup peach yogurt
8 ounces whipped topping

Combine the pudding mix and milk in a blender container. Process for 30 seconds. Blend in the yogurt. Pour into serving cups. Chill for 5 minutes or until serving time. Top with the whipped topping. Yield: 4 servings.

Bridget Lyons, Church Point

Oreo Delight

1 (16-ounce) package Oreo cookies
1/2 cup melted margarine
8 ounces cream cheese, softened
1 cup confectioners' sugar
16 ounces whipped topping
1 (6-ounce) package vanilla instant pudding mix
3 cups milk

Crush the cookies and place in bowl, reserving 1/2 cup of the crumbs for topping. Add the margarine and mix well. Press into a 9x13-inch baking dish. Let stand until cool. Mix the cream cheese, confectioners' sugar and half the whipped topping in a mixer bowl. Spread over the crust. Mix the pudding mix and milk in a bowl. Pour over the cream cheese mixture. Spread with the remaining whipped topping. Sprinkle with the reserved cookie crumbs. Chill until serving time. Yield: 16 servings.

Phyllis G. Moore, Jonesboro

Peach Kuchen

2 cups flour
3/4 teaspoon salt
4 teaspoons baking powder
1/4 teaspoon nutmeg
1/2 cup sugar
1 cup milk
1 egg, beaten
1/4 cup melted butter
1 (21-ounce) can peach pie filling
1/4 teaspoon cinnamon
1 cup sour cream

Combine the flour, salt, baking powder, nutmeg and sugar in a bowl. Add the milk, egg and butter. Stir just until blended. Pour into a greased 2-quart baking dish. Top with the pie filling. Sprinkle with the cinnamon. Bake at 375 degrees for 35 minutes. Spread the sour cream over the top. Bake for 5 minutes longer. Serve warm. Yield: 8 servings.

Dolores Ancelet, Rayne

Pecan Pie Dessert

1 (2-layer) package yellow cake mix
1/2 cup melted margarine
1 egg
1 1/2 cups dark corn syrup
1 teaspoon vanilla extract
3 eggs
1/2 cup packed brown sugar
1 cup chopped pecans

Reserve 2/3 cup of the cake mix. Combine the remaining cake mix with the margarine and egg in a bowl and mix well. Press into a greased 9x13-inch baking dish. Bake at 350 degrees for 20 minutes or until brown. Mix the reserved cake mix, corn syrup, vanilla, eggs and brown sugar in a mixer bowl. Pour over the crust. Sprinkle with the pecans. Bake at 350 degrees for 35 to 40 minutes or until golden brown. Yield: 15 servings.

Reneè L. LaVergne, Elton

Surprise

1/4 cup margarine, softened
8 ounces cream cheese, softened
1/2 cup confectioners' sugar
2 (4-ounce) packages French vanilla instant pudding mix
3 1/2 cups milk
16 ounces whipped topping
1 1/4 pounds Oreo cookies

Combine the margarine, cream cheese and confectioners' sugar in a small bowl. Combine the pudding mix, milk and whipped topping in a large bowl. Process the cookies into fine crumbs in a food processor or crush by hand. Alternate layers of the cream cheese mixture, pudding and crumbs in a large bowl or clean flowerpots until all ingredients are used, ending with the crumbs. May add artificial flowers to flowerpots. Yield 15 servings.

Louise Cater, Rayville

The Best Rice Pudding

1/4 cup seedless raisins
1/4 cup dried sour cherries
1/2 cup uncooked rice
1/2 vanilla bean, split
1/4 teaspoon salt
1 cup boiling water
2 cups milk
1 cup half-and-half
1/2 cup sugar
2 eggs, beaten
1/4 teaspoon ground cinnamon

Plump the raisins and cherries in boiling water in a small bowl. Drain and set aside. Add the rice, vanilla bean and salt to 1 cup boiling water in a saucepan. Cook for 10 minutes. Add the milk, half-and half, sugar, eggs and cinnamon. Cook over very low heat for 10 minutes or until the rice is tender. Stir in the raisins and cherries, discarding the vanilla bean. Pour into a greased shallow 1 1/2-quart baking dish. Bake at 350 degrees for 10 minutes or until lightly browned. Yield: 8 servings.

Evelyn Bieber, Branch

Yam Parfait

1 cup flour
1/2 cup melted butter
1 cup finely chopped pecans
8 ounces cream cheese, softened
1 cup confectioners' sugar
12 ounces whipped topping
2 cups mashed cooked yams
1/4 to 1/2 cup sugar
1 teaspoon vanilla extract
2 to 3 teaspoons cornstarch
1 (12-ounce) can syrup-pack crushed pineapple
1 (4-ounce) package vanilla instant pudding mix

Mix the flour, butter and pecans in a bowl. Press into a 9x13-inch baking dish. Bake at 350 degrees for 20 minutes. Cool completely. Beat the cream cheese with the confectioners' sugar in a mixer bowl until smooth. Blend in 1 cup of the whipped topping. Spread over the cooled crust. Mix the yams with 1/4 to 1/2 cup sugar and the vanilla in a bowl. Stir the cornstarch into the pineapple in a saucepan. Cook until thickened, stirring constantly. Prepare the pudding mix using the package directions. Combine the yams, pineapple and pudding in a bowl and mix well. Spread over the cream cheese layer. Top with the remaining whipped topping. Chill until serving time. Garnish with additional pecans. Cut into squares to serve. Yield: 12 servings.

Vashti Radzikowski, Ringgold

Nutritional Profiles

The editors have attempted to present these recipes in a form that allows approximate nutritional values to be computed. Persons with dietary or health problems or whose diets require close monitoring should not rely solely on the nutritional information provided. They should consult their physicians or a registered dietitian for specific information.

Abbreviations for Nutritional Profile

Cal — Calories	T Fat — Total Fat	Sod — Sodium
Prot — Protein	Chol — Cholesterol	g — Grams
Carbo — Carbohydrates	Fiber — Dietary Fiber	mg — Milligrams

Nutritional information for these recipes is computed from information derived from many sources, including materials supplied by the United States Department of Agriculture, computer databanks and journals in which the information is assumed to be in the public domain. However, many specialty items, new products and processed foods may not be available from these sources or may vary from the average values used in these profiles. More information on new and/or specific products may be obtained by reading the nutrient labels. Unless otherwise specified, the nutritional profile of these recipes is based on all measurements being level.

- **Artificial sweeteners** vary in use and strength so should be used "to taste," using the recipe ingredients as a guideline. Sweeteners using aspartame (NutraSweet and Equal) should not be used as a sweetener in recipes involving prolonged heating which reduces the sweet taste. Refer to package information.
- **Alcoholic ingredients** have been analyzed for basic ingredients, although cooking causes the evaporation of alcohol, thus decreasing caloric content.
- **Buttermilk, sour cream** and **yogurt** are the types available commercially.
- **Cake mixes** preapred using package directions include 3 eggs and 1/2 cup oil.
- **Chicken**, cooked for boning and chopping, has been roasted; this method yields the lowest caloric values.
- **Cottage cheese** is cream-style with 4.2% creaming mixture. Dry curd cottage cheese has no creaming mixture.
- **Eggs** are all large. To avoid raw eggs that may carry salmonella as in eggnog or 6-week muffin batter, use an equivalent amount of commercial egg substitute.
- **Flour** is unsifted all-purpose flour.
- **Garnishes**, serving suggestions and other optional additions and variations are not included in the profile.
- **Margarine** and **butter** are regular, not whipped, or presoftened.
- **Milk** is whole milk, 3.5% butterfat. Low-fat milk is 1% butterfat. Evaporated milk is whole milk with 60% of the water removed.
- **Oil** is vegetable cooking oil. **Shortening** is hydrogenated vegetable shortening.
- **Salt** and other ingredients to taste as noted in the ingredients have not been included in the nutritional profile.
- If a choice of ingredients has been given, the nutritional profile reflects the first option. If a choice of amounts has been given, the nutritional profile reflects the greater amount.

Nutritional Profiles

Pg #	Recipe Title (Approx Per Serving)	Cal	Prot (g)	Carbo (g)	T Fat (g)	% Cal from Fat	Chol (mg)	Fiber (g)	Sod (mg)
11	Beef and Pork Dip	253	18	2	19	67	68	<1	453
12	Broccoli Dip	72	3	3	5	64	10	1	751
13	Chile Corn Dip	159	4	6	13	74	22	<1	277
13	Crab Meat Dip	155	13	4	10	56	56	<1	623
14	Hot Crab Dip	334	25	5	24	64	136	<1	1079
14	Mock Crab Salad Dip	227	16	19	10	40	33	1	1217
15	Crawfish Dip	321	12	5	28	79	107	1	461
15	Easy Crawfish Dip	147	8	5	10	64	67	<1	492
16	Layered Shrimp Dip	131	14	7	5	37	66	1	516
17	Shrimp Rémoulade	115	9	3	7	58	79	<1	246
18	Seafood Cocktail Spread	121	10	3	8	56	76	<1	312
19	Shrimp Spread	233	14	7	17	65	116	1	469
19	Taco Dip	123	4	8	9	62	21	2	375
20	French Bread and Ham Appetizer	191	6	13	13	59	19	1	444
20	Rice Cakes	127	3	18	6	38	0	1	89
21	Sweet Potato Cheese Balls	73	2	8	4	47	8	1	270
22	Tortilla Pinwheels	66	2	4	5	65	12	<1	116
23	Waldorf Sandwiches	115	2	13	7	50	2	1	83
23	Cinnamon Pecans	206	3	11	18	75	0	2	7
24	Eggnog	192	9	22	8	37	176	0	106
24	Easy Punch	80	<1	20	<1	1	0	<1	7
25	Yellow Slush Punch	78	<1	20	<1	<1	0	<1	2
26	Spiced Tea	132	1	33	<1	1	0	<1	12
29	Cauliflower Soup	341	17	13	26	66	77	2	1097
30	Corn Chowder	309	9	42	14	38	27	3	1215
31	Crawfish and Corn Chowder	488	23	63	20	34	121	6	1468
32	Shrimp and Corn Soup	183	14	17	7	35	112	3	522
33	Shrimp and Corn Fest Chowder	326	13	38	14	37	68	2	924
34	Creole Gumbo	183	15	10	10	48	118	3	867
35	Lumberjack Soup	377	18	39	16	37	37	4	1879

Nutritional Profiles

Pg #	Recipe Title (Approx Per Serving)	Cal	Prot (g)	Carbo (g)	T Fat (g)	% Cal from Fat	Chol (mg)	Fiber (g)	Sod (mg)
36	Mirliton and Shrimp Soup	398	30	33	18	39	212	4	491
37	Taco Soup	287	22	26	11	34	56	3	1146
38	Turkey and Sausage Gumbo	185	6	10	14	67	16	1	238
39	Blueberry Salad	472	6	69	21	39	44	2	173
40	Congealed Fruit Delight	351	6	48	16	40	30	1	270
41	Fruit Salad	279	2	64	4	13	0	4	98
42	Fruity Salad	425	6	32	32	66	47	1	162
42	Sour Cream Fruit Salad	336	4	46	17	43	40	1	114
43	Strawberry and Banana Salad	201	3	39	5	22	10	2	57
44	Strawberry Pretzel Salad	219	2	28	12	46	13	1	164
45	Rice and Cranberry Fluff	349	3	48	18	44	0	2	19
46	Harvest Rice Salad	270	4	26	17	55	49	1	1132
47	Crawfish Pasta Salad	597	25	61	28	42	238	2	408
48	Super Chicken Salad	430	25	22	28	57	78	4	509
49	Wilted Lettuce Salad	337	4	22	26	69	31	<1	317
50	Grandma's Potato Salad	180	5	22	9	42	111	1	267
51	Spinach Salad	202	5	30	8	35	31	2	324
52	Marinated Vegetables	441	7	66	19	37	0	7	796
52	Thousand Island Dressing	231	1	3	24	92	46	<1	363
55	Barbecue Beef Sandwiches	163	19	11	5	27	54	1	690
56	Beef Strips with Angel Hair Pasta	410	29	52	9	21	54	4	145
57	Beefy Fettuccini	726	41	38	45	56	127	3	1006
58	Burger Cheese Casserole	574	32	16	42	66	156	1	1453
59	Beef and Cheese Pie	341	26	11	21	57	152	1	497
60	Coal Miner's Pie	436	24	48	17	35	91	5	1553
61	Enchiladas Acapulco*	765	48	56	39	46	138	7	1747
62	Fiesta Beef and Rice	631	40	58	26	37	114	1	1105
63	Real Italian Lasagna	698	54	28	41	53	163	3	1142
64	Beef Lasagna	428	34	24	21	45	92	2	1001
65	Meat and Potato Casserole	625	40	42	33	48	120	3	2139

Nutritional Profiles

Pg #	Recipe Title (Approx Per Serving)	Cal	Prot (g)	Carbo (g)	T Fat (g)	% Cal from Fat	Chol (mg)	Fiber (g)	Sod (mg)
66	Beefy Oyster Dressing	496	41	22	26	48	135	2	311
67	Wagon Wheel Loaf	337	29	16	17	46	116	3	545
68	Best Barbecue Sauce (per cup)	202	2	35	8	33	21	2	1514
69	Creole Pork Chops	314	26	24	12	36	69	3	408
70	Pork Chop and Rice Bake	324	25	26	12	35	69	1	243
70	Black-Eyed Pea Jambalaya	Nutritional information for this recipe is not available.							
71	Easy Oven Jambalaya	298	13	31	13	39	24	1	1051
72	Rice-Cooker Jambalaya	522	17	51	28	48	24	6	1505
73	Sausage Jambalaya	457	28	35	22	44	80	3	1090
74	Breakfast Casserole	397	22	30	21	48	252	2	594
75	Sunday Eggs	289	17	17	18	54	252	1	756
76	Slow-Cooker Teriyaki Venison	201	23	9	8	35	49	<1	6423
77	Deer Tenderloin*	254	24	33	2	9	75	1	40
78	Venison Meat Pies	426	22	27	25	54	68	1	42
79	Venison Patties over Fettuccini	428	29	64	5	11	99	2	241
80	Wild Beast Feast	Nutritional information for this recipe is not available.							
81	Grilled Dove	429	41	7	27	55	169	0	390
82	Delicious Duck	574	26	7	49	77	108	<1	852
83	Chicken Broccoli Cups	476	43	32	22	40	106	2	1289
84	Chicken Casserole	678	42	18	49	65	143	2	853
85	Cheesy Chicken Casserole	725	44	55	37	45	111	4	1548
86	Chicken Creole	239	17	30	6	23	40	2	552
87	Chicken Divan	548	26	34	35	57	81	3	1040
88	Mexican Chicken	470	21	35	28	52	61	4	1410
89	Onion and Cheese Chicken	336	31	6	20	55	102	<1	582
90	Chicken and Rice Casserole	377	31	33	12	30	78	1	982
91	Chicken Spaghetti	610	31	36	38	56	128	2	1374
92	Chicken in Tomato Gravy	294	36	12	11	34	100	4	336
93	Easy Chicken Stew	313	36	8	15	43	109	<1	1002
93	Chicken Casserole/White Beans and Rice	267	31	21	6	22	77	3	834

Nutritional Profiles

Pg #	Recipe Title (Approx Per Serving)	Cal	Prot (g)	Carbo (g)	T Fat (g)	% Cal from Fat	Chol (mg)	Fiber (g)	Sod (mg)
94	Chicken and Dumplings	522	39	37	23	41	105	2	868
97	Baked Fish and Rice	623	52	39	27	40	124	1	1082
98	International Stuffed Catfish	395	29	26	19	44	112	<1	1036
99	Light Catfish Fillets	207	15	3	14	64	86	1	186
100	Fish Court Bouillon	452	44	17	23	46	132	3	307
101	Snappy Garfish	Nutritional information for this recipe is not available.							
102	Poached Shark	509	64	12	21	38	314	1	1632
103	Jann's Alligator Sauce Picante	Nutritional information for this recipe is not available.							
104	RR's Alligator Sauce Picante	Nutritional information for this recipe is not available.							
105	Maw Maw's Crab Meat au Gratin	419	34	8	28	59	240	<1	932
106	Crawfish Casserole	716	30	74	33	41	152	5	1469
107	Crawfish Étouffée	564	23	12	48	76	285	3	641
108	Easy Crawfish Étouffée	283	17	9	19	63	167	2	716
109	Mom's Crawfish Étouffée+	217	21	11	10	41	138	2	734
110	Crawfish Fettuccini Casserole	784	38	44	50	58	207	2	1179
111	Crawfish Pies	422	13	29	28	61	60	1	803
112	Crawfish Quiche	376	22	15	25	61	188	1	454
113	Low-Fat Barbecued Shrimp	347	68	4	4	10	632	<1	894
114	Shrimp Scampi	522	17	1	50	86	229	<1	850
115	Shrimp and Crab Stew+	156	23	2	6	35	156	<1	796
116	Shrimp Étouffée	345	22	26	16	43	158	2	1603
117	Shrimp Fettuccini	630	44	50	53	56	417	1	1350
118	Easy Shrimp Fettuccini	443	22	49	17	35	135	2	350
119	Quick Shrimp and Pasta	276	21	22	11	37	190	1	792
120	Great Seafood Casserole	636	29	38	41	58	170	2	1418
123	Artichokes and Tomatoes	39	2	8	<1	8	1	1	403
124	Low-Fat Asparagus Fettuccini Alfredo	285	17	53	1	2	0	4	873
125	Toledo Bend Baked Beans	586	18	67	30	44	48	15	1302
126	Creole-Style Green Beans	137	6	19	5	31	8	5	1031
127	Bean and Artichoke Casserole	158	7	14	9	48	7	1	1040

Nutritional Profiles

Pg #	Recipe Title (Approx Per Serving)	Cal	Prot (g)	Carbo (g)	T Fat (g)	% Cal from Fat	Chol (mg)	Fiber (g)	Sod (mg)
128	Broccoli Casserole	262	9	12	21	70	20	3	804
129	Cabbage Casserole	265	9	20	17	58	22	3	797
130	Baked Corn	190	6	24	9	41	40	2	438
131	Corn Casserole	196	5	31	8	33	43	2	797
132	Chile Corn Casserole	473	10	38	34	61	67	3	864
133	Granny's Corn Maque Choux	230	3	28	14	49	20	3	323
134	Eggplant and Green Pepper Italian*	180	9	20	8	39	21	6	1569
135	Mirliton Casserole	223	16	18	11	41	42	2	102
136	Mirliton Pirogues	326	16	24	20	52	57	3	477
137	Black-Eyed Pea Casserole	638	35	42	37	52	147	6	1003
138	Poke Salad	118	4	5	10	70	71	2	299
139	Heavenly Hash Brown Casserole	488	12	27	37	67	74	1	853
140	Potato Casserole	397	10	36	25	55	74	2	300
141	Squash Casserole	348	9	26	25	61	12	4	859
142	Spinach and Artichoke Casserole	323	10	13	27	73	54	1	1459
143	Glazed Sweet Potato Casserole	239	3	47	6	20	8	4	48
144	Holiday Sweet Potatoes	482	5	72	21	38	54	3	289
145	Pineapple Sweet Potato Puff	327	6	55	10	27	62	4	165
146	Sweet Potato-Banana Casserole	325	3	54	13	33	23	4	153
147	Restuffed Sweet Potatoes	499	3	74	23	40	62	4	258
148	Zucchini Pie	311	9	16	24	68	61	1	505
149	Green Rice	161	3	25	5	28	0	<1	284
150	Rice and Carrot Dressing	175	3	26	6	18	0	4	109
151	Rice Casserole	461	24	49	18	36	62	2	799
152	Pineapple Casserole	342	5	54	13	33	30	1	229
153	Blueberry Jelly (per tablespoon)	33	<1	9	<1	1	0	<1	<1
153	Sweet Pickles	54	<1	14	<1	1	0	<1	363
154	Bread-and-Butter Pickles (per tablespoon)	16	<1	4	<1	<1	0	<1	200
157	Banana Bread	115	1	17	5	39	18	<1	92
157	Broccoli Corn Bread	218	9	16	13	54	68	2	717

Nutritional Profiles

Pg #	Recipe Title (Approx Per Serving)	Cal	Prot (g)	Carbo (g)	T Fat (g)	% Cal from Fat	Chol (mg)	Fiber (g)	Sod (mg)
158	Mexican Corn Bread	263	11	26	13	45	36	2	429
159	Poppy Seed Bread	176	3	15	12	61	21	1	119
160	Sweet Potato Biscuits	340	5	39	18	48	3	2	736
160	Sweet Potato Muffins	196	3	23	11	48	35	1	156
161	Harvest Bread	82	3	14	1	15	<1	1	168
162	Sausage Bread	305	15	21	18	58	45	1	824
163	Cheese Bread	305	10	28	17	51	23	2	572
164	Dinner Rolls	79	2	12	2	21	4	<1	76
167	Sugarless Applesauce Cake	229	3	31	11	42	27	2	131
168	Banana Cake	192	3	31	7	31	25	1	136
169	Banana Pineapple Cake	433	5	54	23	47	40	2	198
170	Blueberry Cake	313	4	46	13	37	84	1	222
170	Buttermilk Cake	366	5	55	15	36	67	1	62
171	Coconut Dream Cake	359	4	42	21	50	0	2	281
171	Fresh Cranapple Cake	590	6	70	33	49	53	3	174
172	Fig Cake	440	4	53	25	49	40	2	99
173	Italian Cream Cake	809	8	97	45	49	110	3	355
174	Lemon Poppy Seed Cake	158	3	25	5	28	<1	<1	164
175	Mandarin Orange Cake	329	3	53	12	33	30	1	408
175	Old-Fashioned Cajun Syrup Cake	666	8	118	20	26	71	3	315
176	Fresh Peach Cake	485	5	63	24	45	120	1	302
177	Pear Cake	399	4	58	19	41	0	7	230
177	Pineapple Cake	372	5	52	17	40	20	1	492
178	Cream Cheese Pound Cake	460	6	56	24	47	142	1	242
178	Pound Cake	533	7	68	26	44	195	1	275
179	Pumpkin Roll	252	4	34	12	40	74	1	193
180	Red Velvet Cake	403	4	50	22	47	29	1	210
181	Sad Cake	437	4	55	25	49	28	3	293
182	Sweet Potato Cake	658	5	80	37	49	69	2	225
183	So-Good Cake	440	5	59	22	44	76	1	344

Nutritional Profiles

Pg #	Recipe Title (Approx Per Serving)	Cal	Prot (g)	Carbo (g)	T Fat (g)	% Cal from Fat	Chol (mg)	Fiber (g)	Sod (mg)
183	Frosting/German Chocolate Cake (per cup)	1722	20	175	111	56	398	12	561
184	Sugar-Free Apple Pie	310	3	41	16	44	0	3	238
185	French Coconut Pie	419	3	53	23	48	31	2	262
185	Milk Chocolate Candy Bar Pie	689	7	79	41	52	13	3	367
186	Cool Fruit Pies	408	6	48	23	49	24	2	204
186	Candied Pecan Pie	Nutritional information for this recipe is not available.							
187	Best-Ever Pecan Pie	573	5	71	32	49	111	1	326
188	Pecan Fudge Pie	504	6	71	25	42	91	3	319
189	Rich Pecan Pie	546	6	85	22	36	114	1	233
190	Nuttier Pecan Pie	682	7	75	43	54	80	3	229
193	Divinity	120	1	23	3	24	0	<1	33
194	Cocoa Cheese Fudge	445	4	63	21	42	14	1	360
194	Foolproof Dark Chocolate Fudge	188	3	23	11	49	6	2	23
195	Microwave Peanut Brittle	175	3	29	6	31	0	1	136
195	Mircrowave Peanut Butter Fudge	175	3	24	8	41	2	1	92
196	Pecan Delights	60	<1	4	5	72	10	<1	52
196	Pecan Log	403	3	66	16	34	9	3	33
197	Pralines	132	1	17	7	47	5	1	19
197	Sweet Potato Pralines	278	1	44	12	37	13	1	10
198	Yam Candy	76	<1	12	3	37	1	<1	17
198	Toffee Crisps	89	1	6	7	70	10	1	52
199	Brown Sugar Cookies	95	1	10	6	57	6	<1	40
199	Chinese Chews	103	1	18	4	29	18	1	42
200	Chocolate Chip Crisp Cookies	67	1	10	3	40	4	<1	58
200	Forgotten Cookies	44	1	4	3	64	0	<1	3
201	Fannie Farmer Bars	111	1	19	4	31	19	1	74
202	Old-Fashioned Tea Cakes	164	2	20	8	45	18	<1	113
203	Oatmeal Cookies	70	1	9	3	41	6	<1	44
204	Peanut Butter Cookies	131	4	14	7	48	12	1	71
204	Peanut Butter Soybean Cookies	59	2	6	3	48	4	<1	43

Nutritional Profiles

Pg #	Recipe Title (Approx Per Serving)	Cal	Prot (g)	Carbo (g)	T Fat (g)	% Cal from Fat	Chol (mg)	Fiber (g)	Sod (mg)
205	Pecan Fingers	48	<1	4	3	65	5	<1	80
206	Persimmon Cookies	164	2	23	8	40	19	1	77
207	Pfefferneusse	80	1	15	2	19	4	<1	67
208	Best Sand Tarts	98	1	8	7	65	14	<1	1
208	Stir Me Nots	176	2	19	11	54	4	1	93
209	Special Cookies	166	2	24	7	39	19	1	87
210	Frosted Sugar Cookies	75	1	10	4	44	13	<1	67
211	Sugar Cookies	131	1	17	6	44	24	<1	92
211	Whoppers Cookies	132	2	17	7	45	13	<1	95
212	The World's Best Cookie	88	1	10	5	53	7	<1	60
213	Easy Blueberry Cobbler	258	2	49	7	23	2	2	167
213	Banana Pudding	535	6	84	21	35	25	1	431
214	Bread Pudding	253	6	38	9	31	68	1	191
214	Rum Sauce for Bread Pudding	320	1	38	18	49	27	0	209
215	Caramel Bread Pudding	309	8	39	15	42	104	2	194
216	Caramel-Pecan Chesecake	511	9	39	38	64	146	1	269
217	Pineapple Cream Cheesecake	455	5	63	22	42	60	1	353
218	Chocolate Éclair Dessert	302	3	47	12	35	6	1	346
218	Cushaw Dessert	447	2	67	19	39	42	1	228
219	Dutch Babies	262	7	28	14	47	137	1	150
219	Layered Dessert	613	7	51	44	63	29	2	510
220	Lemon Mousse	382	6	52	18	41	7	0	424
220	Oreo Delight	421	4	46	25	53	22	1	463
221	Peach Kuchen	372	7	56	14	33	59	2	474
222	Pecan Pie Dessert	389	4	59	17	37	57	1	365
222	Surprise	453	5	53	26	50	24	1	535
223	The Best Rice Pudding	206	6	31	7	30	73	1	126
224	Yam Parfait	661	6	70	42	55	47	2	293

*Nutritional information does not include oil for frying.
+Nutritional information does not include roux.

Index

ALLIGATOR
Jann's Alligator Sauce Picante, 103
RR's Alligator Sauce Picante, 104
Wild Beast Feast, 80

APPETIZERS. *See also* Dips; Spreads
French Bread and Ham Appetizer, 20
Shrimp Rémoulade, 17
Tortilla Pinwheels, 22

APPLE
Fresh Cranapple Cake, 171
Sugar-Free Apple Pie, 184
Sugarless Applesauce Cake, 167

ARTICHOKES
Artichokes and Tomatoes, 123
Bean and Artichoke Casserole, 127
Spinach and Artichoke Casserole, 142

BANANA
Banana Bread, 157
Banana Cake, 168
Banana Pineapple Cake, 169
Banana Pudding, 213
Strawberry and Banana Salad, 43
Sweet Potato-Banana Casserole, 146

BEANS. *See also* Green Beans
Toledo Bend Baked Beans, 125

BEEF. *See also* Ground Beef
Barbecue Beef Sandwiches, 55
Beef and Pork Dip, 11
Beef Strips with Angel Hair Pasta, 56
Best Barbecue Sauce, 68

BEVERAGES
Easy Punch, 24
Eggnog, 24
Spiced Tea, 26
Yellow Slush Punch, 25

BLACK-EYED PEAS
Black-Eyed Pea Casserole, 137
Black-Eyed Pea Jambalaya, 70

BLUEBERRY
Blueberry Cake, 170
Blueberry Jelly, 153
Blueberry Salad, 39
Dutch Babies, 219
Easy Blueberry Cobbler, 213

BREADS
Banana Bread, 157
Broccoli Corn Bread, 157
Cheese Bread, 163
Dinner Rolls, 164
Harvest Bread, 161
Mexican Corn Bread, 158
Poppy Seed Bread, 159
Sausage Bread, 162
Sweet Potato Biscuits, 160
Sweet Potato Muffins, 160

BROCCOLI
Broccoli Casserole, 128
Broccoli Corn Bread, 157
Broccoli Dip, 12
Chicken Broccoli Cups, 83
Chicken Divan, 87

CAKES
Banana Cake, 168
Banana Pineapple Cake, 169
Blueberry Cake, 170
Buttermilk Cake, 170
Coconut Dream Cake, 171
Cream Cheese Pound Cake, 178
Fig Cake, 172
Fresh Cranapple Cake, 171
Fresh Peach Cake, 176
Italian Cream Cake, 173
Lemon Poppy Seed Cake, 174
Mandarin Orange Cake, 175
Old-Fashioned Cajun Syrup Cake, 175
Pear Cake, 177
Pineapple Cake, 177
Pound Cake, 178
Pumpkin Roll, 179
Red Velvet Cake, 180
Sad Cake, 181
So-Good Cake, 183
Sugarless Applesauce Cake, 167
Sweet Potato Cake, 182

CANDY. *See also* Fudge
Divinity, 193
Microwave Peanut Brittle, 195
Pecan Delights, 196
Pecan Log, 196
Pralines, 197
Sweet Potato Pralines, 197

Index

Toffee Crisps, 198
Yam Candy, 198

CATFISH
Fish Court Bouillon, 100
International Stuffed Catfish, 98
Light Catfish Fillets, 99

CAULIFLOWER
Cauliflower Soup, 29

CHEESECAKES
Caramel-Pecan Cheesecake, 216
Pineapple Cream Cheesecake, 217

CHICKEN
Cheesy Chicken Casserole, 85
Chicken and Dumplings, 94
Chicken and Rice Casserole, 90
Chicken Broccoli Cups, 83
Chicken Casserole, 84
Chicken Casserole with White Beans and Rice, 93
Chicken Creole, 86
Chicken Divan, 87
Chicken in Tomato Gravy, 92
Chicken Spaghetti, 91
Easy Chicken Stew, 93
Mexican Chicken, 88
Onion and Cheese Chicken, 89
Super Chicken Salad, 48

COOKIES
Best Sand Tarts, 208
Brown Sugar Cookies, 199
Chinese Chews, 199
Chocolate Chip Crisp Cookies, 200
Fannie Farmer Bars, 201
Forgotten Cookies, 200
Frosted Sugar Cookies, 210
Oatmeal Cookies, 203
Old-Fashioned Tea Cakes, 202
Peanut Butter Cookies, 204
Peanut Butter Soybean Cookies, 204
Pecan Fingers, 205
Persimmon Cookies, 206
Pfefferneusse, 207
Special Cookies, 209
Stir Me Nots, 208
Sugar Cookies, 211
The World's Best Cookie, 212
Whoppers Cookies, 211

CORN
Baked Corn, 130
Broccoli Corn Bread, 157
Chile Corn Casserole, 132
Chile Corn Dip, 13
Corn Casserole, 131
Corn Chowder, 30
Crawfish and Corn Chowder, 31
Granny's Corn Maque Choux, 133
Mexican Corn Bread, 158
Shrimp and Corn Fest Chowder, 33
Shrimp and Corn Soup, 32

CRAB MEAT
Crab Meat Dip, 13
Great Seafood Casserole, 120
Hot Crab Dip, 14
Maw Maw's Crab Meat au Gratin, 105
Mirliton Pirogues, 136
Mock Crab Salad Dip, 14
Seafood Cocktail Spread, 18
Shrimp and Crab Stew, 115

CRAWFISH
Baked Crawfish Fettucini, 110
Crawfish and Corn Chowder, 31
Crawfish Casserole, 106
Crawfish Dip, 15
Crawfish Étouffée, 107
Crawfish Fettuccini Casserole, 110
Crawfish Pasta Salad, 47
Crawfish Pies, 111
Crawfish Quiche, 112
Easy Crawfish Dip, 15
Easy Crawfish Étouffée, 108
Mom's Crawfish Étouffée, 109
Wild Beast Feast, 80

DESSERTS. *See also* Cakes; Candy; Cheesecakes; Cookies; Pies; Puddings
Chocolate Éclair Dessert, 218
Cushaw Dessert, 218
Dutch Babies, 219
Easy Blueberry Cobbler, 213
Layered Dessert, 219
Oreo Delight, 220
Peach Kuchen, 221
Pecan Pie Dessert, 222
Surprise, 222
Yam Parfait, 224

Index

DIPS
Beef and Pork Dip, 11
Broccoli Dip, 12
Chile Corn Dip, 13
Crab Meat Dip, 13
Crawfish Dip, 15
Easy Crawfish Dip, 15
Hot Crab Dip, 14
Layered Shrimp Dip, 16
Mock Crab Salad Dip, 14
Taco Dip, 19

EGG DISHES
Breakfast Casserole, 74
Sunday Eggs, 75

FILLINGS
Cream Cheese Filling, 179
Creamy Butter Filling and Topping, 176

FISH. *See also* Catfish
Baked Fish and Rice, 97
Poached Shark, 102
Snappy Garfish, 101

FROSTINGS
Coconut Cream Cheese Frosting, 182
Cream Cheese Frosting, 173
Creamy Butter Filling and Topping, 176
Frosting for German Chocolate Cake, 183
Lemon Glaze, 174
Red Velvet Frosting, 180

FRUIT. *See* Individual Kinds; Salads, Fruit

FUDGE
Cocoa Cheese Fudge, 194
Foolproof Dark Chocolate Fudge, 194
Microwave Peanut Butter Fudge, 195

GAME. *See also* Alligator; Venison
Delicious Duck, 82
Grilled Dove, 81
Wild Beast Feast, 80

GREEN BEANS
Bean and Artichoke Casserole, 127
Creole-Style Green Beans, 126

GROUND BEEF
Beef and Cheese Pie, 59
Beef Lasagna, 64
Beefy Fettuccini, 57
Beefy Oyster Dressing, 66
Black-Eyed Pea Casserole, 137
Burger Cheese Casserole, 58
Coal Miner's Pie, 60
Enchiladas Acapulco, 61
Fiesta Beef and Rice, 62
Meat and Potato Casserole, 65
Mirliton Casserole, 135
Real Italian Lasagna, 63
Rice Casserole, 151
Sausage Jambalaya, 73
Taco Soup, 37
Wagon Wheel Loaf, 67

GUMBO
Creole Gumbo, 34
Turkey and Sausage Gumbo, 38

HAM
French Bread and Ham Appetizer, 20

JAMBALAYA
Black-Eyed Pea Jambalaya, 70
Easy Oven Jambalaya, 71
Rice-Cooker Jambalaya, 72
Sausage Jambalaya, 73

JELLIES
Blueberry Jelly, 153

LASAGNA
Beef Lasagna, 64
Real Italian Lasagna, 63

MICROWAVE
Onion and Cheese Chicken, 89
Peanut Brittle, 195
Peanut Butter Fudge, 195

MIRLITON
Mirliton and Shrimp Soup, 36
Mirliton Casserole, 135
Mirliton Pirogues, 136

OYSTERS
Beefy Oyster Dressing, 66

PASTA. *See also* Salads, Pasta
Baked Crawfish Fettucini, 110
Beef Strips with Angel Hair Pasta, 56
Beefy Fettuccini, 57

Index

Cheesy Chicken Casserole, 85
Chicken Spaghetti, 91
Crawfish Fettuccini Casserole, 110
Easy Shrimp Fettuccini, 118
Lowfat Asparagus Fettuccini Alfredo, 124
Quick Shrimp and Pasta, 119
Shrimp Fettuccini, 117
Venison Patties over Fettuccini, 79

PEANUT BUTTER
Microwave Peanut Butter Fudge, 195
Peanut Butter Cookies, 204
Peanut Butter Soybean Cookies, 204

PICKLES
Bread-and-Butter Pickles, 154
Sweet Pickles, 153

PIES
Cool Fruit Pies, 186
Milk Chocolate Candy Bar Pie, 185
French Coconut Pie, 185
Sugar-Free Apple Pie, 184

PIES, PECAN
Best-Ever Pecan Pie, 187
Candied Pecan Pie, 186
Nuttier Pecan Pie, 190
Pecan Fudge Pie, 188
Rich Pecan Pie, 189

PORK. *See also* Ham; Sausage
Beef and Pork Dip, 11
Beefy Oyster Dressing, 66
Best Barbecue Sauce, 68
Creole Pork Chops, 69
Pork Chop and Rice Bake, 70
Venison Meat Pies, 78

POTATO
Grandma's Potato Salad, 50
Heavenly Hash Brown Casserole, 139
Meat and Potato Casserole, 65
Potato Casserole, 140

POULTRY. *See* Chicken; Turkey

PUDDINGS
Banana Pudding, 213
Bread Pudding, 214
Caramel Bread Pudding, 215
Lemon Mousse, 220
Rum Sauce for Bread Pudding, 214
The Best Rice Pudding, 223

RICE
Baked Fish and Rice, 97
Chicken and Rice Casserole, 90
Chicken Creole, 86
Chicken Divan, 87
Crawfish Casserole, 106
Easy Oven Jambalaya, 71
Fiesta Beef and Rice, 62
Great Seafood Casserole, 120
Green Rice, 149
Harvest Rice Salad, 46
International Stuffed Catfish, 98
Pork Chop and Rice Bake, 70
Rice and Carrot Dressing, 150
Rice and Cranberry Fluff, 45
Rice Cakes, 20
Rice Casserole, 151
Rice-Cooker Jambalaya, 72
Sausage Jambalaya, 73
The Best Rice Pudding, 223

SALADS, DRESSINGS
Thousand Island Dressing, 52

SALADS, FRUIT
Blueberry Salad, 39
Congealed Fruit Delight, 40
Fruit Salad, 41
Fruity Salad, 42
Rice and Cranberry Fluff, 45
Sour Cream Fruit Salad, 42
Strawberry and Banana Salad, 43
Strawberry Pretzel Salad, 44

SALADS, MAIN DISH
Super Chicken Salad, 48

SALADS, PASTA
Crawfish Pasta Salad, 47

SALADS, VEGETABLE
Grandma's Potato Salad, 50
Harvest Rice Salad, 46
Marinated Vegetables, 52
Spinach Salad, 51
Wilted Lettuce Salad, 49

SANDWICHES
Barbecue Beef Sandwiches, 55

Index

Waldorf Sandwiches, 23

SAUSAGE
- Breakfast Casserole, 74
- Easy Oven Jambalaya, 71
- Rice-Cooker Jambalaya, 72
- Sausage Bread, 162
- Sausage Jambalaya, 73
- Turkey and Sausage Gumbo, 38
- Wild Beast Feast, 80

SEAFOOD. *See* Crab Meat; Crawfish; Fish; Oysters; Shrimp

SHRIMP
- Easy Shrimp Fettuccini, 118
- Great Seafood Casserole, 120
- Layered Shrimp Dip, 16
- Lowfat Barbecued Shrimp, 113
- Mirliton and Shrimp Soup, 36
- Quick Shrimp and Pasta, 119
- Seafood Cocktail Spread, 18
- Shrimp and Corn Fest Chowder, 33
- Shrimp and Corn Soup, 32
- Shrimp and Crab Stew, 115
- Shrimp Étouffée, 116
- Shrimp Fettuccini, 117
- Shrimp Rémoulade, 17
- Shrimp Scampi, 114
- Shrimp Spread, 19

SIDE DISHES
- Beefy Oyster Dressing, 66
- Best Barbecue Sauce, 68
- Blueberry Jelly, 153
- Green Rice, 149
- Pineapple Casserole, 152
- Rice and Carrot Dressing, 150
- Rice Casserole, 151

SNACKS
- Cinnamon Pecans, 23
- Rice Cakes, 20
- Waldorf Sandwiches, 23

SOUPS
- Cauliflower Soup, 29
- Corn Chowder, 30
- Crawfish and Corn Chowder, 31
- Lumberjack Soup, 35
- Mirliton and Shrimp Soup, 36
- Shrimp and Corn Fest Chowder, 33
- Shrimp and Corn Soup, 32
- Taco Soup, 37

SPINACH
- Spinach and Artichoke Casserole, 142
- Spinach Salad, 51

SPREADS
- Seafood Cocktail Spread, 18
- Shrimp Spread, 19
- Sweet Potato Cheese Balls, 21

SWEET POTATO
- Glazed Sweet Potato Casserole, 143
- Holiday Sweet Potatoes, 144
- Pineapple Sweet Potato Puff, 145
- Restuffed Sweet Potatoes, 147
- Sweet Potato-Banana Casserole, 146
- Sweet Potato Biscuits, 160
- Sweet Potato Cake, 182
- Sweet Potato Cheese Balls, 21
- Sweet Potato Muffins, 160
- Sweet Potato Pralines, 197

TURKEY
- Turkey and Sausage Gumbo, 38

VEGETABLES. *See also* Individual Kinds; Salads, Vegetable
- Artichokes and Tomatoes, 123
- Cabbage Casserole, 129
- Eggplant and Green Pepper Italian, 134
- Lowfat Asparagus Fettuccini Alfredo, 124
- Poke Sallet, 138
- Rice and Carrot Dressing, 150
- Squash Casserole, 141
- Zucchini Pie, 148

VENISON
- Deer Tenderloin, 77
- Slow-Cooker Teriyaki Venison, 76
- Venison Meat Pies, 78
- Venison Patties over Fettuccini, 79
- Wild Beast Feast, 80

Louisiana Temptations
Louisiana Farm Bureau Women
P.O. Box 95004
Baton Rouge, Louisiana 70895-9004

Please send me _____ copies of **Louisiana Temptations** at $16.95 per copy plus ($3.55) postage and handling.

Enclosed you will find my check or money order for $ ___________

Name ____

Address ____

City_________________________ State ___ Zip Code __________

Louisiana Temptations
Louisiana Farm Bureau Women
P.O. Box 95004
Baton Rouge, Louisiana 70895-9004

Please send me _____ copies of **Louisiana Temptations** at $16.95 per copy plus ($3.55) postage and handling.

Enclosed you will find my check or money order for $ ___________

Name ____

Address ____

City_________________________ State ___ Zip Code __________

Louisiana Temptations
Louisiana Farm Bureau Women
P.O. Box 95004
Baton Rouge, Louisiana 70895-9004

Please send me _____ copies of **Louisiana Temptations** at $16.95 per copy plus ($3.55) postage and handling.

Enclosed you will find my check or money order for $ ___________

Name ____

Address ____

City_________________________ State ___ Zip Code __________

Louisiana Farm Bureau Federation, Inc.
P.O. Box 95004
9516 Airline Highway
Baton Rouge, Louisiana 70895-9004
504-922-6200